MW01094370

CARNIVAL
IN LOUISIANA

Leopard masker on New Orleans' Canal Street welcomes
all the world to Carnival in Louisiana.

(Louisiana Office of Tourism)

CARNIVAL

IN LOUISIANA

Celebrating Mardi Gras
from the French Quarter to the Red River

BRIAN J. COSTELLO

LOUISIANA STATE UNIVERSITY PRESS
BATON ROUGE

Published by Louisiana State University Press
Copyright © 2017 by Louisiana State University Press
All rights reserved
Manufactured in the United States of America
First printing

Designer: Michelle A. Neustrom
Typefaces: Adobe Garamond Pro, text; Tribute, display
Printer and binder: McNaughton & Gunn, Inc.

Library of Congress Cataloging-in-Publication Data

Names: Costello, Brian J., author.
Title: Carnival in Louisiana : celebrating Mardi Gras from the French Quarter to the Red
   River / Brian J. Costello.
Description: Baton Rouge : Louisiana State University Press, [2017] | Includes bibliographical
   references.
Identifiers: LCCN 2016041284| ISBN 978-0-8071-6652-9 (cloth : alk. paper) | ISBN 978-0-
   8071-6653-6 (pdf) | ISBN 978-0-8071-6654-3 (epub) | ISBN 978-0-8071-6655-0 (mobi)
Subjects: LCSH: Carnival—Louisiana. | Louisiana—Social life and customs.
Classification: LCC GT4210.L8 C66 2017 | DDC 394.2509763—dc23
   LC record available at https://lccn.loc.gov/2016041284

To all those who have made Carnival in Louisiana
possible each year: those untold individuals and groups
behind the scenes and behind the masks who have provided
the inspiration, time, talent, and financial resources for
the perpetuation and promotion of the state's
signature celebration. *Merci beaucoup.*

Spanish Town parade-goers vie for throws
cast from floats in Baton Rouge's longest parade.
(Courtesy Amanda M. Scallan)

CONTENTS

CONTENTS

Photographs follow page 102.

PREFACE

The aim of *Carnival in Louisiana* is to provide a historical summary of, comparison between, and thorough-as-possible listing of the various Carnival festivities currently held in Louisiana. The large number of events in the state makes it difficult, if not impossible, to give due attention to every parade, ball, and other celebration. For well-documented parades and balls dating back a century or more, the task is relatively easy. Including events that are only a year or two old, or more spontaneous and low-key in organization, requires more research. Regardless, for the benefit of would-be revelers, readers should come to appreciate the diversity of present-day Carnival festivities in Louisiana and their history.

The book is organized by geographic/cultural region to survey the areawide festivities that a particular destination offers. New Orleans, the "Carnival City," and its suburbs remain unparalleled in the age, scope, distinction, and variety of their pre-Lenten events. Southwest Louisiana encompasses the cities of Lafayette, Lake Charles, Houma, and Thibodaux, whose street parades are more or less similar to those of New Orleans. Smaller communities of Acadiana host the incomparably colorful rural Courir de Mardi Gras.

Southeast Louisiana includes the old Creole French town of New Roads; the relatively new-to-parading capital city of Baton Rouge; the Florida Parishes cities of Hammond, Mandeville, Covington, Slidell, and more; and the towns in the River Parishes bordering the Mississippi between Baton Rouge and New Orleans. The parades of Central and North Louisiana—specifically the Alexandria, Monroe, and Shreveport regions—while younger in age than most of the southern festivities, are growing in number and popularity and resemble the New Orleans pattern but with less emphasis on the secrecy of old-line Carnival.

This volume relies principally on the author's thirty-odd years of personal research in archival and contemporary print-news sources and, to a lesser extent, krewe histories. Both of these types of resources have consistently elaborated on the details of the festivities, including each year's parade themes, number of floats and bands, crowd estimates, weather conditions, and parade incidents. Direct quotes are referenced by endnotes; general information, by abbreviated sources at the end of each part division. Full sources are listed in the bibliography.

The author extends sincere gratitude to LSU Press acquisitions editor Margaret H. Lovecraft, with whom researching, crafting, and illustrating a book of this scope was a joy as well as a privilege and a learning experience. She joined me, my wife, Mary, and my family in "field research" in the form of attending Mardi Gras parades and related indoor festivities, which proved to be as fun as they were informative.

Special thanks are offered to the photographers and agencies who loaned their images to help illustrate the text: Country Lane Photography, Margaret H. Lovecraft, Amanda M. Scallan, Laura R. Gleason, Brandon M. Dufrene, Will Avera, Mary J. Langlois, Matthew Noel for the Houma Area Convention and Visitors Bureau, Amy Lynn Treme and Jim Noetzel for the Shreveport Convention and Tourist Bureau, the Krewe of Janus, the *Pointe Coupee Banner,* Slidell Mardi Gras Museum, Iberville Parish Library, Alexandria-Pineville Convention and Visitors Bureau, the State Library of Louisiana, and the Louisiana Office of Tourism. Gratitude is also extended to those patient individuals who assisted in the considerable task of locating, selecting, and receiving permissions for the photos: Arriollia "Bonnie" Vanney, Charlene Bonnette, Norris Fontenot, Mary Catherine R. LaCour, Barbara M. Hebert, Erin L. Rolfs, Jeff Richard, Chris Jay, Joey Pierce, and Tamie Fingleton.

Finally, to my wife, Mary, *bien merci* for supporting my varied Carnival commitments through the years and this newest manifestation of my lifelong love of and dedication to the preservation and promotion of Louisiana's Carnival traditions.

CARNIVAL
IN LOUISIANA

Introduction
Ancient Origins, Louisiana Adaptations

The state of Louisiana, known the world over for its history, folklore, and *joie de vivre,* plays host each year to one of the greatest celebrations on the globe: the pre-Lenten Carnival and its climax, Mardi Gras. Carnival has been celebrated for many centuries and in various forms, including public masquerading, dancing, and parading in the predominantly Latin, Catholic countries of Europe. These merriments were introduced into the culture of the New World by southern European settlers in the Gulf Coast, the Caribbean, and Central and South America.

In Louisiana, many persons have only to hear the words *Carnival* or *Mardi Gras* and their minds are filled with images of the elaborate parades, balls, and other festivities held in Greater New Orleans. To many others, the words will just as soon bring to mind the smaller pre-Lenten celebrations throughout Louisiana: parades in Lafayette, New Roads, Houma, and Thibodaux; the traditional Courir de Mardi Gras at Mamou; the zaniness of the Spanish Town parade truck floats in Baton Rouge; boat parades in the Florida Parishes; and the increasingly popular pre-Lenten festivities established in recent years in the central and northern parts of the state. From the French Quarter on the Mississippi River to Shreveport on the Red River, Carnival in Louisiana today includes every region of the state, to the delight of residents and visitors alike.

The Carnival season and Mardi Gras day trace their roots from the Bacchanalia and Saturnalia ritual promiscuity of Roman times. With the spread of Christianity, similar revelry occurred during the period of Carnival (Latin for "farewell to the flesh"), which extended from Twelfth Night (January 6, the feast of the Epiphany of Christ) to Shrove Tuesday (the day before Ash Wednesday and the ensuing forty-day penitential season of Lent). In France, Shrove Tuesday came to be known as Mardi Gras or "Fat Tuesday," a reference to the daylong feasting before the Lenten fast. The date of Mardi Gras depends on the date of Easter, which may fall as early as March 22 or as late as April 25. Lent, in turn, numbers forty days, excluding the six Sundays occurring during the season. Mardi Gras, therefore, may fall as early as February 3 or as late as March 9.

The words *Mardi Gras* and *Carnival* have come to be used interchangeably, though there are inherent semantic differences in the terms. Carnival is a season—the entire program of balls, parades, and other merrymaking from January 6 to Shrove Tuesday. Mardi Gras is but one day—Fat Tuesday. Louisianans and visitors alike often refer to the entire season, which can vary in length from twenty-eight to sixty-three days, as "Mardi Gras" and to the final day of the season as "Carnival Day" or "Mardi Gras Day."

Carnival and Mardi Gras are concepts that have been engrained on the Louisiana psyche since the earliest days of the state's historical record. On Fat Tuesday (March 3) 1699, when Canadian explorers led by Pierre Le Moyne, Sieur d'Iberville, camped beside a small bayou while on their journey up the Mississippi River, the group christened the smaller stream "Bayou de Mardi Gras" and the area "Pointe du Mardi Gras" in honor of the festivities they had known in Canada and France. The Rex organization, New Orleans' most recognized Carnival association, erected a plaque on this site in 1999 in observance of the three-hundredth anniversary celebration of Iberville's expedition to Louisiana.

A French soldier named Nicholas Langlois is said to have established the first Carnival organization in the Louisiana colony, the Société de Saint-Louis, at Fort Conde (present-day Mobile, Alabama) in 1704. One of the first known Mardi Gras masquerades recorded in the immediate New Orleans area was an impromptu one, staged in 1730 and recorded by noted chronicler Marc-Antoine Caillot. As clerk of the French Company of the Indies, a corporation having considerable holdings and investments in the Louisiana colony, Caillot and his associates decided to observe Lundi Gras by crashing a wedding celebration on Bayou St. John, in the rear of New Orleans. Dressed in various fashions of burlesque, and accompanied by musicians, the party arrived at the wedding reception by light of flambeaux and added much to the festivity of the evening. By 1743, Carnival balls were being held in more elegant fashion in New Orleans. But when Louisiana passed from French to Spanish control in 1763, the new government prohibited public masking. A law of 1781 expressly barred persons of color from masking. After the brief return to French rule in 1800 and the ultimate transfer to American rule in 1803, the public observance of Carnival resumed in Louisiana.

New Orleans' pre-Lenten balls increased in number, some of which were remembered in oral history as particularly elaborate events. Early scholars on the subject contend that in 1827 a group of young New Orleans men, recently returned from their studies in Paris, donned costumes and made a raucous cacophony upon musical instruments, cowbells, and dishpans en route to a ball in the city's Vieux Carré, or French Quarter. Such "promiscuous" masking by groups and individuals increased during the 1830s. In 1835, revelers donned improvised heads of beasts and fantastic characters and then paraded on horseback, on foot, and in animal-drawn conveyances while making music and shouting.[1]

Documentation of organized groups parading the streets of New Orleans on Mardi Gras dates from the 1830s. As maskers walking alongside or riding aboard large allegorical "cars" or floats were a traditional feature of European Carnival celebrations, it was logical that New Orleanians would adopt this custom as well. Remembering Shrove Tuesday 1835, James R. Creecy gave one of the first descriptions of a float and its characters in New Orleans: "One large nondescript car drawn by 4 horses uniquely caparisoned and draped with fiery dragons, scorpions, et cetera was the moving prison of the devil chained securely—horns, tail and all—blowing from his mouth flames of fire and sulphur—surrounded by imps and devils whooping, yelling and gibbering."[2]

From 1841 to 1844, cavalcades of maskers costumed as Bedouins delighted New Orleanians who thronged the streets and packed French

Quarter balconies for Mardi Gras. For some reason or another, the Bedouins failed to appear in 1845, and the Creole press began to fear the end of a beautiful tradition. By the late 1840s, Mardi Gras in New Orleans had degenerated into a dangerous day with increasing reports of small boys, many in everyday clothes, tossing flour, then dust and quicklime, and, finally, bricks at those few maskers and spectators who dared to venture outside.

Meanwhile, "American"—or Protestant, Anglo-Saxon—southerners were beginning their own traditions of parading. Mardi Gras celebrations had been held by the Creoles of Mobile, Alabama, since the days of French colonial rule, but it was not until the later antebellum period that the custom of parading in the streets gained hold there. Elaborate New Year's Eve parades of maskers were held in Mobile beginning in 1830, and in 1840 decorated, animal-drawn floats were introduced into the lineup. The earliest of Mobile's parading groups, composed of Anglo-Saxon citizens, was known as the Cowbellion de Rakin Society, the first of the many "mystic societies" to parade in that city's history.

The debate continues into the twenty-first century as to whether New Orleans or Mobile stages the oldest Carnival celebrations and which was the "original" home of Mardi Gras. Both cities raise valid points in their favor, but large-scale parades of floats on Shrove Tuesday were first observed in New Orleans, suggesting that this city, the undisputed Mardi Gras City, has a longer Carnival parade tradition. On their part, Mobilians keep fast to and promote their city's status as the "Mother of Mystics," or first city to have secret Carnival organizations and merriments.

In 1857, six former Cowbellions of Mobile and thirteen Anglo-Saxon men of New Orleans formed the city's first "krewe"—or established organization—to parade in the Crescent City, that of Comus. Following the Civil War and the return to a sense of normalcy, other parading krewes were founded in New Orleans: the Twelfth Night Revelers, Rex, the Knights of Momus, and the Krewe of Proteus. Though each of these

4

krewes is ruled by a king chosen each year, the king of Rex has the honor of being "King of the Carnival," or supreme monarch of the season.

For every Carnival devotee from Louisiana and beyond, the colors purple, green, and gold are as familiar as all-American red, white, and blue. According to Carnival historian Arthur Hardy, the king of the Rex krewe selected purple, green, and gold as his signature colors for his inaugural parade in 1872 thus: "While they were probably chosen simply because they looked good together and they followed the rules of heraldry, Rex assigned a meaning to each in his 1892 parade, entitled 'Symbolism of Colors.'"[3] Purple symbolizes justice; green, faith; and gold, power—all royal attributes.

The five pioneer krewes were all composed of white males from the upper levels of society who maintained their anonymity from the general public as regards their membership and roles in the parades and balls. At great monetary expense, in the form of annual dues and special assessments, the krewe members entertained New Orleanians and visitors alike with parades of magnificent papier-mâché floats built according to fantastic themes. Like their twenty-first-century counterparts, they wore full-face masks and, in addition, elaborate costumes. Unlike all but a few of the Carnival parades of the late twentieth and early twenty-first centuries, the grand parades of yesteryear were intensely cerebral in subject material and featured little tossing of trinkets (or "throws") to the spectators.

A far cry from today's crowds in casual attire clamoring—often aggressively—for plastic trinkets, the thousands of spectators of all ages from around the country who thronged the city's streets in the nineteenth and early twentieth centuries came dressed in their best and sedately lined the routes to silently take in the splendor of the floats, maskers, and accompanying brass bands. Period news accounts attest that parade viewers frequently clapped appreciation for the passing spectacle and murmured audibly as to the meaning of the bewildering subjects and characters rolling past them.

Twelfth Night Revelers paraded for only a brief period, but its four fellow krewes have parading histories lasting for more than a century. Comus, Momus, and Proteus krewes paraded at night, as had Twelfth Night. Only Rex, King of the Carnival, and his krewe have paraded by day. For illumination, each float in the night parades was circled by dancing flambeaux bearers, usually African American men hired for the occasion and wearing white, full-length robes and cowls. The night parades were each led by a masked king who bore the name of the krewe (that is, Comus, instead of *the King of* Comus) and whose identity remained forever secret to the public. Only Rex is made known to the public, and he has always been chosen from familiar and prominent businessmen and professionals, particularly those who have contributed to civic welfare and humanitarianism.

These "old-line" parade and ball krewes of New Orleans were—and continue to be—intensely discriminating in membership as well as in guest lists to the balls. Only the most prominent businessmen and financiers of New Orleans and the great plantation owners of the surrounding rural parishes were members. As such, they comprised the casts of the entertainments, and chose the royalty to preside and the debutantes to be presented during each season's fetes. Carnival and the social and debutante season have always been synonymous in New Orleans and Louisiana, and therefore the males of the state have largely determined who is to be honored and included—or not—in the balls and related festivities.

With the exception of a few short-lived krewes organized by men of more average means and station, the vast majority of the New Orleans population had little chance of participating in a parade or ball. In the twentieth century, however, the increase in financial stability for many New Orleanians—of both sexes and various ethnicities—caused exponential growth in the number of Carnival krewes presenting parades and/or balls, both in the city proper and in its suburbs. In essence, an employee or trades-/craftsman unknowingly viewing his employer or client as king of a grand nineteenth-century-founded krewe could himself be king and/or have his daughter rule as queen of a newer krewe on another day in any given Carnival season. New Orleans' parading krewes are required, both by their own rules and city ordinance, to remain masked and, at least superficially, anonymous throughout their parades in order to continue the traditional mystique of the celebration.

Though all of New Orleans' krewes have maintained varying degrees of membership requirements, those formed after the post–World War I era were less discriminating than the aristocratic, white, male krewes founded during the nineteenth century. Zulu, the first African American parading krewe, was founded in 1909, and Venus, the first krewe of parading females, debuted in 1941. Zulu originally limited their route to the predominantly African American neighborhoods near North Rampart Avenue, yet thousands of white citizens and visitors flocked to witness the annual parade from the earliest years. Zulu's popularity increased even more with their standardized route, including St. Charles Avenue and Canal Street in the 1960s. At the other extreme, Carnival traditionalists were shocked when the ladies of Venus took to the streets aboard twelve floats rented from the Krewe of Babylon, considering public masking aboard floats a male prerogative. The ladies' charm and the beauty of the floats vanquished the chauvinism, however, and thousands of spectators attended the annual Venus parade until dropping membership numbers spelled the end of the krewe after the 1992 procession. Venus' absence remains one of the most lamented losses of the annual festivities.

The growth in the number of balls and parades spilled over into the adjacent suburban parishes of St. Bernard, Jefferson, and St. Tammany following World War II. To invoke late Louisiana governor Huey P. Long's motto "Every man a king," it seemed as though anyone had a chance of being a king or queen. The number of parades in Greater New Orleans peaked at an all-time high of sixty-four in 1990. Many of the newer krewes were, however, short-lived organizations that held but a few parades and/or balls. The Krewe of Clones, which first marched in 1978 in the French Quarter, was popular for its avant-garde designs and adult themes. In 1973, the city had banned full-scale Carnival parades from the constricted streets of the French Quarter due to the growth in size of floats and crowds. The Krewe de Vieux in 1987, with its miniature floats and with maskers mainly on foot, succeeded the Krewe of Clones, thus preserving in the city's historic center a sense of Carnival in its oldest public form.

Increasingly in the last decades of the twentieth century, the New Orleans Carnival celebration came to be viewed nationwide as a two-week drunken orgy. Promiscuity flourished, and youthful visitors to the city went to great and often lewd lengths to obtain beads, krewe-logo-imprinted cups, doubloons, and other throws cast by the maskers aboard the floats. Television and print media chronicled such activity with even more attention than they allotted for the organized, family-friendly parades.

Krewes whose members had limited personal funds pursued various means of fundraising for the enormous costs of the annual parades and balls, including public bingo games, poker-card "runs," and raffles. The introduction of full-fledged casino gaming, video-poker outlets, and lotteries in New Orleans and elsewhere in Louisiana in the late twentieth century, however, led to the shrinking of those former revenues. As a result, many krewes scaled back their presentations, merged with other krewes, or tried other means to cut costs, only to ultimately disband. St. Bernard Parish's Carnival scene was especially hard hit, falling from a high of more than a dozen parades to a mere two by the early twenty-first century.

New Orleans Carnival aficionados, including the widely known Henri Schindler and Arthur Hardy, have lamented the general decline in the creativity of New Orleans' parades in the second half of the twentieth century. Whereas the city's oldest krewes continued to build their floats fresh each year, the majority of the newer krewes rented their floats from one of the city's huge commercial float pools. Consequently, as in other parading cities of Louisiana and Alabama, the same floats were seen in multiple parades every year with few modifications to suit the krewes' broad themes.

The passage in 1991 of controversial anti-discrimination laws spearheaded by New Orleans city councilwoman Dorothy Mae Taylor required private clubs and parading krewes served by city security, sanitation, and other operations to open their membership to minorities, or at least prove that they did not discriminate in soliciting members. In response, the ancient krewes of Comus and Momus canceled their 1992 parades and have not returned to the streets, limiting their celebrations to private balls. Proteus did not parade from 1992 to 1999, but it resumed the tradition in 2000 to great acclaim from connoisseurs of classic nineteenth-century Carnival artistry.

The terrorist attack of September 11, 2001, affected tourism for years in America's largest cities, including New Orleans. The Carnivals of 2001–5 saw progressively diminishing crowds, though rainy weather during the 2003–5 celebrations was also a cause for sparse attendance.

Then came Katrina. A city that had weathered tropical hurricanes and floods throughout its history experienced its greatest calamity in the form of category 4 Hurricane Katrina on August 29, 2005. Declared the biggest natural disaster in American history, Katrina's storm surge breached levees and flooded 80 percent of New Orleans up to twenty feet deep. Nearby St. Bernard and Plaquemines parishes and the Mississippi Gulf Coast were devastated, and more than 1,800 persons were killed in Louisiana, Mississippi, and Alabama. Hurricane Rita, just one month later, poured more water into the slowly drying Crescent City and stalled recovery even longer. The evacuation and diaspora of three-quarters of the New Orleans–area population remained keenly felt a decade after the disaster, with the pre-Katrina population numbers still not restored.

Many of the Carnival traditions remained, however, and most of New Orleans' krewes turned out with abbreviated parades in 2006, the normal twelve-day parading calendar being scaled back to eight days as a means of reducing security and sanitation costs to the bankrupt city. Though only 125,000 residents had returned to the city at the time, an estimated 400,000 people lined the route of the Rex parade. The New Orleans Convention and Visitors Bureau estimated that 700,000, or 70 percent of the "normal size" Carnival crowds, were in attendance during the five-day, Friday–Fat Tuesday climax. Crowds grew in subsequent years so that by 2009, Fat Tuesday's attendance was pegged at 800,000 and that for the season was back to one million.

A decade after Katrina, many New Orleans krewes had increased membership and were throwing even more trinkets than in the past. Most growth occurred in the "superkrewes," organizations with thousands of members riding dozens of huge, animated, neon- and fiber optic-lighted floats and tossing increasingly elaborate throws to the frenzied masses below. Guest celebrities in the superkrewe parades included professional entertainers and athletes as well as national heroes. Significantly for Carnival traditionalists, a marked return to creativity was also seen as the oldest krewes engaged the talents of distinguished artists such as New Orleans' Henri Schindler to design floats in the whimsical and painstaking style of the nineteenth-century pageants. The period also saw an increase in the number of smaller, neighborhood-based parades of maskers, sometimes accompanied by small floats whose creativity rivaled that of the older and larger organizations.

In a pattern begun before Hurricane Katrina and continued afterward, many of New Orleans' parades held in neighborhoods away from the city center switched their routes to the standard Uptown route of Napoleon and St. Charles avenues, and St. Charles and Canal streets. The parade organizers did so in order to gain the attention of the larger crowds who customarily favor the Uptown route, while city officials realized a reduction in security and sanitation expenses. Thus, krewes such as Alla, Carrollton, and Mid-City, who once paraded exclusively or originally in their own areas, retained their names but rolled with larger attendance on the Uptown route.

Back-to-back scheduling of parades on any given day or night proved a benefit to spectators as well as krewes, the more-is-better attitude being widely held by parade-goers. However, it became more difficult for krewes to obtain large numbers of local marching bands or to reschedule their parades in cases of inclement weather. Thus, fewer parades featured an equal number of marching bands and floats than in past years with the old-line parades. New Orleans krewes supplemented their float lineups with military and ROTC units as well as dance troupes. The latter expanded to include not only squads of teenage schoolgirls but also groups of middle-aged women and coed units. Among others were the Camel Toe Lady Steppers, Pussyfooters, Sirens, Cherry Bombs, Bearded Oysters, Muff-A-Lottas, Rollin' Elvi, and 610 Stompers. The divergence of these groups from the traditional marching-unit image reflects Carnival's ability to adapt and to do so to public acclaim.

Carnival Spreads across Louisiana

In the 1870s and 1880s, the success and allure of New Orleans' annual Carnival parades spurred parading interest in cities far beyond predominantly Creole French South Louisiana. Memphis, St. Louis, Baltimore, Cincinnati, and New York City were among the largely Anglo-Saxon metropolises that staged parades with elaborate floats. Several of those parades were held well outside the pre-Lenten Carnival season, making them neither Mardi Gras nor Carnival parades in the strictest sense. The sponsoring organizations for these parades were short-lived enterprises, and owing to the great costs involved and public ambivalence about such a "foreign" concept as Carnival, the parades were soon discontinued.

Writing in 1890 Mobile, journalist and author T. C. De Leon noted with admirable sharpness: "The Carnival, like the orange and the magnolia, thrives properly only along the shores of the Mexican Gulf. There it was born out of the wedding of Taste and Poetry; there it has lived its beautiful—and in some regard we shall see, its useful—existence, to the ripe maturity of three score years!"[4]

At the time of De Leon's writing, Carnival celebrations in New Orleans and Mobile were large-scale, well-attended annual events, and the Carnival fever had spread throughout predominantly French South Louisiana. Many Louisiana families of means and interest attended or followed news reports of the New Orleans Carnival season, and they were inspired to organize parades, balls, and related festivities in their own communities. Those smaller cities and towns were not strangers to Carnival traditions, though, as costuming by lone and group maskers in the rural areas of South Louisiana had begun in early times.

As in New Orleans, costuming elsewhere in the state demonstrated wide variations in elaborateness and cost. The most economical disguises, as remembered in the early and mid-1900s on the streets of Lafayette, Houma, New Roads, and in rural locales, included gorilla costumes made of Spanish moss as well as old and tattered men's suits or long underwear adorned with strips of cloth or crepe paper or bottle caps. Both men and women might also wear dresses or suits covered in multicolored patches. A masker in wildly mismatched colors was usually referred to—and continues to be so by older observers—simply as a "Mardy Graw."

Whether homemade of wire and papier-mâché or store bought, masks of the old days had an expressionless, somewhat frightening aspect. Adult male maskers, especially in remote, rural areas, often brandished bullwhips, cracking them and frightening children while commanding them to say their prayers. The presence of bullwhips in the context of Carnival may be a vestige of the ritualistic flagellation of merrymakers and penitents in the Lupercalia Carnival of ancient Rome. Older residents of South Louisiana shared childhood memories of wanting to approach Mardi Gras maskers on streets or rural byways for a better view of their costumes, only to flee in terror from the whip-cracking characters.

In the 1800s, wealthy South Louisianans staged Carnival balls, often "fancy dress" (that is, costume and mask) events, in plantation homes and community halls. These were invariably invitation-only affairs. Rural inhabitants of Acadiana—that portion of South Louisiana west of the Atchafalaya River and heavily populated by the "Cajun" descendants of the Acadian French exiles—staged Mardi Gras fais-do-dos, informal community dances named for the expression "go to sleep." Entire families attended these dances, including babies, who were cared for in side rooms away from the frenzy of the dance floor by matriarchal babysitters who admonished their little charges: "fais-do-do!"

By the 1880s, citizens of the preponderantly Francophone towns of South Louisiana who were unable or unwilling to take in the Crescent City's already famous Carnival festivities began to stage their own organized parades. Among the communities holding parades during the late nineteenth and early twentieth centuries were Lafayette, Opelousas, St. Martinville, Bayou Cane, Houma, Thibodaux, New Iberia, Abbeville, Donaldsonville, Plaquemine, New Roads, Marksville, and several towns in St. Tammany Parish. Mule-drawn floats of varying elaborateness—some manufactured by New Orleans' creative firms—as well as local brass bands were the chief attractions. Parades also included revelers on horseback and hilarious maskers on foot. During the early 1900s, decorated automobiles were introduced into the lineup. Many of these parades were followed by masked "fancy dress" balls. In some towns where there were no public celebrations of Carnival, private balls were held in honor of the season.

As in the Crescent City, costumed kings ruled over the small-town parades, bearing the titles "Rex," "Komus [sic]," or "Momus" after New Orleans' monarchs or "King Sucrose" for South Louisiana's sugar industry. These rural monarchs, in the fashion of Rex in New Orleans, often appeared in medieval costume and were described as sovereigns from faraway lands who visited South Louisiana for each year's festivities, usually arriving by river or bayou steamboat to head the parades and preside over the balls.

Since the early 1900s, many Louisiana communities have adopted and discontinued public Carnival celebrations. The number of parades grew exponentially and, while the earliest ones tended to be staged on Shrove Tuesday proper, most by the close of the 1900s were being held on the two weekends prior to the big day.

Among the oldest continuously staged parades outside New Orleans —all held on Mardi Gras itself—are those in New Roads (since 1922),

Lafayette (since 1934), Houma (since 1947), and Franklin (since 1948). Other cities and towns which featured parades in the early twentieth century have since discontinued them and limited their observances to Carnival balls.

In the twenty-first century, the best-attended Shrove Tuesday celebrations in Louisiana outside New Orleans continue to be in Lafayette, where published estimates by parade and law-enforcement officials have run as high as 250,000, and in New Roads and Houma, with estimated attendance of 100,000 each. The full impact of these numbers becomes clear alongside Lafayette's normal population of about 124,000; Houma's, 34,000; and New Roads', smallest of the trio, 6,000. Visitors from nearby Baton Rouge as well as southwestern Mississippi (where no parades roll on Shrove Tuesday) make up the sizable crowd in New Roads.

Other Louisiana cities and towns with long Carnival parade histories have experienced drops in attendance due to the exponential growth of new parades that draw people elsewhere. Predominantly Anglo-Saxon and Protestant Central and North Louisiana began to stage Carnival parades in the latter part of the twentieth century, but most of their citizens likely did not participate in Carnival activities until they were established in their own locales. In cities holding multiple parades on the weekends prior to Mardi Gras as well as on the big day itself—such as Lafayette and Houma—the Shrove Tuesday crowds are often no longer the largest of the season. Revelers who attend an early parade may opt not to attend those on Mardi Gras itself, especially not in inclement weather. Many families choose to attend parades early in the season and use the long Mardi Gras holiday from school—usually Lundi Gras, Mardi Gras, and Ash Wednesday, and in some parishes, the entire week—to travel out of state, with snow skiing and theme parks being popular alternatives.

Everyone in Louisiana Loves a Parade

Parades outside Greater New Orleans generally follow the pattern set there. Krewes, whether of male, female, or mixed membership, ride adaptable rental floats in the major parades of Lafayette, Houma, Thibodaux, Baton Rouge, and other cities and towns of the state. In communities such as New Roads and Franklin, the parades are civic in nature, with floats built anew and manned each year by schools, churches, families, and organizations in a spirit of communal fellowship. These floats are often entered on a competitive basis, with panels of celebrity judges awarding prizes to the most creative entries. Such floats are often elaborate in materials and detail, sometimes sporting mechanical features, and their riders don costumes, masks, and headdresses that reflect their floats' themes.

Among the newer and most spontaneously organized parades in the rural areas of Louisiana, the word "float" is loosely applied to any wheeled vehicle pulled by another. In addition to rented or specially built floats, such conveyances include farm wagons, the flatbeds of trucks and hay trailers, and even boats pulled on trailers—all with a minimum of decoration. Such parades usually include all-terrain vehicles, automobiles, and equestrian groups, and emphasis is placed on the tossing of throws and a general *laissez les bon temps rouler* ("let the good times roll") spirit rather than elaborate floats and costumes.

Interspersed among the floats and lending cadence to the parades of the smaller cities and towns are marching bands and drill units from schools and universities, military units, and dance teams from near and far. Open vehicles bearing krewe captains and court members, grand marshals, celebrity guests, and beauty queens appear in many parades as well. Often bringing up the rear are the home-built "truck floats," large vehicles whose flatbeds are decorated to one degree or another and bear rollicking maskers and the blaring music of bands or sound systems playing classic rock, rhythm and blues, zydeco, Cajun, reggae, and traditional Carnival music.

And then there are the throws. Carnival parades in even the smallest of Louisiana's towns feature plastic bead necklaces and small candies. Most krewes throw thousands of mass-produced doubloons, cups, small toys, and other souvenirs bearing the name and crest of their organization, its date of establishment, and the date of that particular parade. As on Canal Street and St. Charles Avenue in New Orleans, crowds flock to the routes of the state's smaller parades, vying for throws as if the plastic baubles are treasures beyond price.

Most of the state's older and larger krewe parades are led by a king or queen accompanied by pages. In parades led by a king, the queen usually reviews the parade from the krewe's grandstand—the epicenter of the parade route—and here she is toasted by the parading king. In parades led by a queen, the pattern is reversed. Identities of the kings and queens of most parades outside New Orleans are made public before parade time. However, in a few parades, notably those in New Roads, the identities of the kings and queens are kept secret until the parades reach the reviewing stands for unmasking ceremonies. A few krewes in larger communities such as Houma have adopted the concept of parades *without* royalty in order—insiders attest—to lessen costs to the organizations and potential royalty, as well as to eliminate family competition and conflict over who should be chosen.

Under comfortable conditions, or in subfreezing temperatures and rain, millions of Louisianans and visitors from around the globe attend the Carnival parades in New Orleans and across the state each year. In the twenty-first century, parade-goers can—and do—follow weather forecasts and plan their agendas from the slew of scheduled events accordingly. In earlier years, however, revelers took their chances in braving the elements to view the few parades of the era, often enduring severe conditions. Comus' 1914 parade, "Tales of Chaucer," rolled despite sleet and the mercury hovering at 32 degrees Fahrenheit. The *New Orleans Picayune* of the following day—Ash Wednesday—reported that throngs defied the uncompromising weather, stating how "the press [of the crowd on lower St. Charles Avenue] seemed greater than in previous years" and that as Comus, the king, himself rounded Lee Circle into St. Charles Street, his gaze was met by "a sea of bobbing heads."[5]

The worst weather has often caused parades to be postponed, but only on a few known occasions were parades rescheduled beyond the Carnival season. In 1899, the Krewe of Proteus, thwarted by snow, rolled on the first Friday of Lent; in 1990, the Krewe of Alla rolled on St. Patrick's Day; and in 2005, the Krewe of Amani-Hannibal in Patterson, avoiding forecasts of rain, moved its parade to the first Saturday after Easter.

Mardi Gras 1989—February 7—is notorious as the coldest Shrove Tuesday in living memory, with a range of 26–29 degrees Fahrenheit recorded for the New Roads parades, which were the northernmost to roll that year. Countless roads and bridges were closed throughout the state in anticipation of icy conditions, and only the most intrepid of revelers saw the Mardi Gras parades in New Orleans and the smaller cities and towns that day. The weather for Mardi Gras 2014 was both cold and wet, with predawn snowflakes giving way at daybreak to freezing rain that continued into mid-afternoon. New Roads had a temperature that barely rose from 32 to 34 degrees. The Fat Tuesdays of 1986 and 1978 were slightly warmer, though the latter celebration was also marked by sleet at midday in Lafayette and New Roads. Snow fell in New Orleans on the days leading up to Mardi Gras in 1899, and on Fat Tuesday itself, Rex paraded in a high of only 28 degrees. Snow also fell on New Orleans parades on the second Friday night before Mardi Gras in 1988. At the other extreme, the warmest Mardi Gras celebrations on record were those of February 27, 1917, and February 9, 1932, when on both occasions the mercury soared to a summerlike 83 degrees in New Orleans.

For many generations, lyrical journalists of the Carnival parades personified parade-time rainfall as "Jupiter Pluvius," for the god of rain. This formidable foe has paid many an unwelcome call to Louisiana's Carnival celebrations. In worst-case scenarios, the parades are canceled. Usually, however, they are postponed if the Carnival calendar permits, or they simply roll in the rain. In several instances, individual floats have rolled without riders, owing to inclement weather. Rex has been rained on many times during the parade's history but canceled only once due to the weather: during the rain-soaked 1933 celebration. More recently, Rex paraded three hours late on the rainy Shrove Tuesday of 1995. New Orleans' wettest Mardi Gras on record is that of 1927, when 2.12 inches of rain fell. Topping this figure was New Roads in 2011: dangerously strong winds and lightning and a record 2.88 inches of rain delayed the start of the town's second parade by more than an hour.

Several of New Orleans' Carnival parades have also changed their usual dates to accommodate other large-scale city events. In 2002 and 2013, for example, New Orleans played host to the Super Bowl, and krewes adjusted their schedules in order to decrease congestion in the city and strain on security and sanitation forces.

Accidents—some humorous, others more serious—have dogged many Carnival parades through the years. In New Orleans' and Houma's old night parades, illuminated by torchlight, quite a few floats burned down to the trailer when flambeaux accidentally touched the flammable float materials. Such mishaps occurred in New Orleans to the "Triumph of Typhoeus" float in the Momus parade of 1904, the "Rings of Gyges" in the 1913 Comus parade, and "Glinda's Book of Oz" in the 1947 Cynthius parade. In 1966, a smoking device built into the Batmobile on the "Bat Man" float in the New Roads Lions Carnival parade accidentally caught fire. Though the children aboard were taken off safely, the float burned down to the trailer as it was towed through four more blocks of massed spectators to the nearest fire station.

Breakdowns occurred in the days when mules pulling floats slipped and fell, breaking the wagon shafts, and the floats had to be abandoned. This happened with the "Golden Gates" float in the 1882 Comus parade and the "Silver" float in Momus' parade of 1947. Momus had a second consecutive year of bad luck, as in 1948 the tall rear portion of the throne float ran afoul of a low-lying power line. The back part of the float was torn off, but the king rolled on unperturbed.

In Houma's parades during the 1940s and 1950s, mules drawing floats caused a great deal of mischief—veering into light poles, breaking the wagon shafts, or simply refusing to move. By 1952, all of the state's Carnival parades had forsaken the unpredictable mules for more practical tractors, jeeps, trucks, or cars. Most krewes now hire pools of tractors to draw their floats, with the number of tractors exceeding the floats in case of problems. Personal accidents have included riders falling from floats to their injury—sometimes fatal—on the pavement below. More comical incidents include one smaller city's king toasting in beer instead of the usual proffered champagne, and another monarch whose royal pants fell down while he offered his own champagne toast. Both occurred in the 1980s.

In their rich variety, the Carnival parades, balls, and other merriments staged in New Orleans and in the cities, towns, and rural communities of Louisiana reflect, preserve, and celebrate the state's cultures. Traditional or satirical, lavish or makeshift, long or short, the annual parades continue to be the most recognizable elements of Carnival and to manifest Louisianans' creativity, love of pageantry and mirth, and, perhaps above all, their undeniable *joie de vivre* that make the Mardi Gras State unlike any other in America.

PART I

NEW ORLEANS

For generations, the unique pre-Lenten Carnival celebration of fantasy, pomp and madcap, and sometimes risqué antics has drawn hundreds of thousands of revelers annually to New Orleans and its suburbs. The street parades are the main attraction—allegorical floats bearing costumed and masked characters who toss souvenir trinkets as a symbol of noble *largesse* to the masses of spectators.

Beginning in the nineteenth century, the main Carnival parades in New Orleans were staged by the krewes of Comus, Rex, Momus, and Proteus. Of these, only Rex and Proteus continue to parade in the twenty-first century, though all four original krewes were integral to the establishment of a distinct Louisiana Carnival tradition and together set the standard for subsequent merrymaking organizations.

From the old-line four's pattern of parades and balls blossomed ethnic, socioeconomic, and aesthetic variations, including the Mardi Gras Indians, walking clubs, "superkrewes," and other forms of revelry. As a result, twenty-first-century Carnival in New Orleans offers something of interest for all parade-goers, whether participants or spectators.

1

The Old-Line Four
Comus, Rex, Momus, and Proteus

The Mistick Krewe of Comus, whose name reflects both Old English spelling of the word "crew" and John Milton's epic mythological hero, established the custom of krewe-sponsored Carnival parades with its premiere pageant of two flambeaux-encircled allegorical floats on Mardi Gras night 1857. Since that time, Carnival—long celebrated in Latin Europe, the Caribbean, and the Americas—has counted among its most colorful and distinctive celebrations those of New Orleans and the state of Louisiana.

Rolling with the theme "Paradise Lost" and followed by a tableau ball, the first Comus parade grew quickly and attracted increasingly large crowds despite the Creole press's initial resentment of the krewe's Anglo-Saxon membership. After Comus' fifteen-float parade of 1861, the krewe sat out the remainder of the Civil War years during the Federal occupation of New Orleans. Comus returned in 1866 with a pageant of figures on foot, followed by a similar procession in 1867, both owing to limited finances. The extraordinary 1867 parade, entitled "The Triumph of Epicurus," featured maskers costumed as all the bounty of a banquet plus the table appointments, led by Comus the king on horseback. A prominent feature of the parade was the Boeuf Gras, or "Fat Ox," much like the oxen paraded prior to butchering and cooking in France's Mardi Gras observances.

Floats were reintroduced into the lineup by the time of the 1869 parade, and the length of the annual procession grew steadily thereafter. Comus' longest parades were those of 1872 and 1874, both of which stretched with twenty-five floats. From 1882 until 1933, all of Comus' parades rolled with twenty floats, each a masterpiece in conception and execution by the most talented of local artists. There was no parade in 1875, however, due to escalating political tensions of postbellum Reconstruction in the city, and for several years in the 1880s due to financial difficulties.

Comus paraded in severe weather in 1899, with a temperature of 38 degrees Fahrenheit; in 1909, which was marked by a rainstorm; and in 1914, when frigid temperatures mingled sleet with rain. Comus' pluckiness in 1909 was reported in the following day's *Picayune*: "When the pageant was in St. Charles Street, near Canal, the sheets of water borne on the breath of a strong wind, deluged men and cars [floats] alike. But all the while the dripping maskers danced and sported on their cars, Comus waved his goblet to the throngs under the sheds and the soaked musicians kept step to the suggestive strains of 'It Looks to Me Like a Big Night To-Night.'"[1] That same night, the krewe's captain was said to have fined one of the maskers a hundred dollars for daring to open an umbrella for protection, the action being deemed ungallant and spoiling the pristine beauty of the display.

Comus chose his first queen, Miss Mildred Lee, to share his throne at the post-parade ball of 1882. Subsequent queens have included Miss Winnie Davis, daughter of the late Confederate president, Jefferson Davis, in 1892, and a succession of prominent debutantes. Comus' successful Mardi Gras night parades spurred the organization of other krewes in New Orleans. The Twelfth Night Revelers, named for the day on which they rolled (January 6), paraded every year during 1870–76, with the exception of 1875. The Revelers' last parade stretched with thirty-three floats, and the krewe limited its activities thereafter to balls only.

The most recognized symbol of New Orleans Carnival the world over is Rex, the King of Carnival. His colorful pageant has taken the Crescent City by festive storm on Shrove Tuesday morning for nearly a century and a half. Rex is the only old-line Carnival monarch whose identity is made public—and, indeed, publicized—as he is invariably chosen from among the city's most influential businessmen and benefactors. Ever since Rex made his debut on Mardi Gras afternoon 1872, he has always been socially deferential to his older kinsman, Comus. Beginning in 1882 and continuing into the twenty-first century, the grand finale of Carnival in Louisiana has been the visit made by Rex and his queen and court to the ball of Comus, thereby paying homage to the oldest Carnival king. Lewis J. Salomon reigned as the first Rex in 1872 but had no queen. In 1873, Rex, in the person of E. B. Wheelock, chose as his queen Mrs. Walker Fearn. Beginning the following year with Miss Margaret Maginnis, unmarried young ladies have reigned as Queen of Carnival. Since Rex's inaugural year, the tune "If Ever I Cease to Love" has been the organization's official anthem. Lydia Thompson and her burlesque troupe were in New Orleans at the time and performed the song, whose nonsensical lines include a reference to Grand Duke Alexis Romanov, another visitor to New Orleans' 1872 Carnival festivities.

Rex, like his contemporaries, did not parade in 1875, owing to civil unrest in the city. When the King of Carnival reappeared in 1876, he rode on a float for the first time. Behind him stretched a line of marchers reportedly three miles long. Rex presented his first formal parade of floats in 1877, when rainfall failed to diminish the spectacle of twenty-five floats built around the theme "Military Progress of the World." Twenty-nine floats rolled in 1878; the parades of 1879 through 1894 included from nineteen to twenty-three floats. From 1895 until the second half of the twentieth century, Rex rolled each year with twenty floats, the lineup always being interspersed with numerous marching bands. More recently, the Rex parade has included twenty-seven floats, including the King's throne car, followed by the Boeuf Gras, the King's Calliope, and the Royal Jester.

Whereas Rex's earliest parades were triumphal and/or comic in execution, those of 1883 to the present have consisted of beautiful floats depicting scenes of history, mythology, literature, fantasy, and other subjects. Gradually banned from the rear of Rex's train were the individual maskers and advertising wagons that were features of the King of Carnival's earliest appearances; they were supplanted in the 1930s by separate truck parades. After the parade of 1901, the Boeuf Gras was not to be seen in Rex's annual pageants for many years, the parade organizers having decided that the presence of the animal was unbecoming to Rex's increasingly elaborate parades.

The earliest Kings of Carnival were dressed in the styles of ancient warrior-rulers of Egypt, Persia, and the Teutonic realms. By the close of the nineteenth century, Rex dressed as a medieval European monarch: in tunic and hose, with false hair, mustache, and beard; rouged cheeks; wearing a jeweled crown and brandishing a scepter; and with a generous train flowing from his shoulders. This hirsute and jolly image became so popular that most Carnival monarchs in New Orleans and as well as smaller Louisiana cities paraded in similar robes and accessories all through the twentieth century and into the twenty-first. By contrast, the gowns of Carnival queens, both in New Orleans and in smaller cities, have mirrored the fashions of the times: the hourglass silhouette and tiny crowns of the late nineteenth and early twentieth centuries; the flapper-length frocks worn with full trains and towering crowns during the 1920s; full-skirted gowns during the 1950s; and the sylphlike, magnificently hued medieval robes and trains of the late twentieth and early twenty-first centuries.

Another of the grand nineteenth-century Carnival krewes, the Knights of Momus, premiered with a New Year's Eve parade in 1872 but switched to parading on the Thursday night preceding Mardi Gras in 1876. Momus, God of Mockery and the Night, chose as his first queen Miss Elise McStea for the ball of 1881. With the lapse in parading by Comus due to financial difficulties, Momus moved to Mardi Gras–night parading; he, his queen, and his court received visits from Rex and the Queen of Carnival at the post-parade balls in 1883 and 1885. Because of the krewe's own financial difficulties, Momus held no parades for several years, including the stretch from 1888 to 1899, but rolled most years from 1900 through 1991 on the Thursday night before Mardi Gras.

In the nineteenth and early twentieth centuries, Momus usually presented parades of great artistic beauty, choosing themes from literature, history, and the arts. Its 1877 parade, however, held during continued Reconstruction-era political tensions, was pure satire. With the theme "Hades: A Dream of Momus," the krewe portrayed local and national political figures as animals, causing great scandal and a return to more graceful themes in subsequent parades. The second half of the twentieth century was marked by Momus' return to the satirical but in more lenient taste than its 1877 presentation, with pokes at local political figures and controversies.

Like his kinsman Comus, Momus retired from parading after the 1991 procession rather than comply with the city ordinance requiring Carnival organizations to prove that they did not discriminate in membership requirements and admissions. Momus has continued to stage its annual ball, a highlight of the season. Meanwhile, the satirical Krewe of Chaos, formed in 2001 and rolling in Momus' former Thursday-night time slot, employs the old Momus float chassis. Chaos' riders are said to include many Momus members, thereby continuing the old krewe's tradition of entertaining the general public.

The Krewe of Proteus first rolled in 1882 and, aside from some lapses through the years, has provided parades and balls of exquisite beauty into the twenty-first century. While the Comus parade was noted for its classic beauty and literary themes and the Momus parade for its often comic or satirical elements, the annual procession of Proteus came to be known for the whimsical style of its floats, even in the portrayal of dramatic or tragic subjects. Unlike his older kinsmen, Proteus selected a queen—Miss Ida Taylor—to share his reign at his very first ball. Proteus, God of the Sea, made his Crescent City premiere on Lundi Gras night with seventeen floats depicting "Ancient Egyptian Theology." The floats in the annual pageant gradually increased to twenty by 1893, the number that continues to roll today. From 1886 to 1889, Proteus took advantage of the absence of Comus and paraded in the latter's stead on Mardi Gras night, each time receiving the homage of Rex and his court at the close of the festivities.

In 1890, Comus returned to the streets, and both Comus and Proteus rolled on Shrove Tuesday evening. The masked captains of these two proud krewes nearly came to blows as their parades collided on Canal Street that historic night, but a disguised spectator, later revealed to be the brother of Proteus' captain, led his sibling out of the path of Comus' captain. The Comus parade rolled into the French Quarter, with Proteus following behind. In 1891, both of the krewes rolled again on the same night, but without collision and without incident. In 1892, the Proteus organization reverted to its customary Monday-night schedule.

Proteus has been plagued with more bad weather than any other parading krewe in American Carnival history. In 1899, when a record snow-and-ice storm gripped Louisiana, Proteus' parade and ball were postponed until the next Friday night. This and Alla's postponed parade of 1990, which was delayed until St. Patrick's Day, are the only known occasions when Carnival festivities were held during Lent. Proteus' 1927 parade completed only half of its route, never making it to Canal Street, owing to a downpour that drenched floats and riders alike. Two noble krewes, the Twelfth Night Revelers and the High Priests of Mithras, came to the rescue, providing Proteus and his retainers with dry costumes for the Sea God's ball that night. In subsequent years, heavy rainfall prevented Proteus from parading altogether six times: in 1933, 1940, 1952, 1955, 1973, and 2004.

Proteus likewise remained in his den from 1993 through 1999, as did his kinsmen Comus and Momus, in the wake of the city's passage of its anti-discrimination ordinance. The Sea God's annual tableau balls, however, like those of Comus and Momus, continued to form a glittering highlight of New Orleans' social season while the respective kings refrained from their street parades. Both residents and visitors to the Crescent City greeted the resumption of the Proteus parade on its traditional Monday night in 2000 with wide acclaim. With Proteus' return to the streets, the total number of krewes that rolled in the light of the old-fashioned flambeaux rose to eight. The magic of the Sea God, enthroned on his signature giant-seashell float, preceded by his captain and lieutenants and followed by his loyal krewemen, is a high point of the

Carnival season, and the annual Protean spectacle continues as the only night parade founded in the 1800s to march in the new century.

After their parades of 1917, Momus, Proteus, Rex, and Comus stayed off the streets in deference to World War I and its aftermath, returning one at a time between 1920 and 1924. The krewes also remained in their headquarters, or "dens," from 1942 to 1945 (World War II) and in 1951 (Korean conflict). Comus scaled back its number of floats from twenty to seventeen, and Momus sat out for several years in the 1930s, both in response to diminished finances and membership loss in the lean years of the Great Depression. In 1979, a citywide police strike caused the old-line four, as well as nine other krewes, to cancel their parades.

Newspaper accounts of the opening decades of the twentieth century refer to Momus, Rex, and Comus float riders as sporadically casting "souvenir favors" or "throws" to individuals lining the parade routes. These incidents appear to have been personal rather than krewe-wide acts of the riders. In 1920, however, Rex began to feature the throwing of favors by all float riders, perhaps in an effort to enliven the crowds, who that year were restrained by the rigors of Prohibition. Other krewes followed suit, and the public, in addition to admiring the passing parades, came to expect thrown trinkets or candy. The dynamic of the Carnival parade had changed.

Rex's throws in 1920 consisted of bubble gum, candy, crackerjack, and—appropriately for that cold, rainy day—cough drops. In succeeding years, the Carnival King's retainers rewarded the crowds with necklaces of colored-glass beads, bracelets, and other glittering ornaments. In 1960, Rex became the first krewe to mint commemorative metallic coins, or "doubloons"—the invention of local artist H. Alvin Sharpe—that have since become a standard throw in most Louisiana Carnival parades. Doubloons, like plastic go-cups and some of the more elaborate necklaces cast by the float riders, commonly feature the krewe's logo as well as its theme for the current year's parade.

During the 1920s, Proteus joined his kinsmen in throwing trinkets to the spectators lining the parade route. The sea god and krewe, however, concentrated more on the opulence of their floats and costumes than on their quantity of throws. Along with the customary compliments on the beauty of the procession, there were shouts of "Stingy" and "Tightwad" from the public.

The ever-increasing cries of "Throw me something, Mister," from spectators have resulted in exponential growth in the quality and quantity of throws cast in Carnival parades. Necklaces of glass beads, imported from Czechoslovakia, were thrown in parades of the 1960s, but these were soon replaced with the safer plastic necklaces, which have become increasingly longer with bigger beads. Since the latter decades of the twentieth century, the major crewes have competed with one another in a quest to throw larger and more diverse trinkets. Spectators, in turn, have become less interested in the grandeur of floats and costumes and more consumed with greed for items tossed by the maskers.

2

The Zulu Social Aid and Pleasure Club

R obert Tallant, in his landmark 1948 work *Mardi Gras,* included a
comment by a member of the Zulu Social Aid and Pleasure Club
that symbolizes one of the most festive traditions of American Carnival:
"You see, we Zulus know how to have fun. We get better every year. You
come around and see us next Mardi Gras. Man, that's gonna' be the best
of all!"[1]

According to Zulu's oral tradition, this remarkable krewe traces its
origins to the first days of 1909, when a group of laborers called "the
Tramps" witnessed an acting group called the "Smart Set" perform a
musical comedy skit titled "There Never Was and Never Will Be a King
Like Me" at the Pythian Theater. The characters played members of one
of Africa's most noted tribes, the Zulus, and provided inspiration for the
Tramps to begin a Mardi Gras parading tradition.

Zulu's staff, however, surmises that the krewe's roots are even deeper
and that the club originated with one of New Orleans' many benev-
olent-aid societies. Such organizations, several of which survive today
in New Orleans and in outlying cities and towns, provide monetary
benefits to their members in times of illness and death, the funds being
raised through assessment of dues. The group of men who became the
Zulus are believed to have marched as early as 1901 but emerged officially as "Zulu" in 1909. Originally a walking parade, the celebration
added mule-drawn floats to the lineup in 1915, and in the following year
the krewe was incorporated as the Zulu Social Aid and Pleasure Club.

In 1909 the first Zulu king, William Story, wore a lard-can crown
and brandished a banana-stalk scepter. Subsequent Zulu kings, like

their retainers, wore grass skirts, wigs, and black thermal underwear and blackened their faces to lampoon whites' conception of Zulu warriors. King Zulu's comic presentation was seen as a parody of the splendor of Rex and his krewe, who, in turn, emulated the royal courts of Europe. Taking the parody one step further, Zulu began in 1917 to arrive in the Carnival City early on Mardi Gras morning via tugboat on the now-filled-in New Basin Canal, mimicking Rex's entry via the Mississippi River on Lundi Gras.

Of all the Zulu kings, the most famous was native New Orleans jazz legend Louis Armstrong, who ruled over the chilly 1949 festivities. Zulu kings are elected by their fellow krewe members and are usually prominent business and professional men of the city's African American community. Zulu then selects his queen, and for the past two decades the Zulu kings who are married have selected their wives for the honor. Young college-age ladies of distinction form the court. In 1933, Zulu chose his first queen, Miss Mamie Williams. For many years, each year's Zulu queen greeted her king from a grandstand at the Gilbert Geddes funeral home on Jackson Avenue. Later in the twentieth century, the queens began to ride in the parade, on a float directly following the king's.

Though Zulu and his queen reign supreme over the parade, other perennial characters of great popularity among spectators include the Big Shot, the Witch Doctor, the Ambassador, the Mayor, the Provident Prince, the Governor, Mister Big Stuff, and the king's personal guard, known as the Soulful Warriors. King Zulu and his retainers have become famous for their sometimes vigorous tossing—now more sedately handing out—of decorated coconuts to the spectators lining the route. Some African Americans through the years have thought the costumes and antics of Zulu and his merry men to be undignified, but the overall reception of the paraders has grown exponentially. As early as 1928, the *Louisiana Weekly,* a local African American newspaper, estimated 150,000 persons witnessed the Zulu parade that year.

The move for racial integration and increased pride in African American identity in the early 1960s affected Zulu's membership, as the krewe's web site explains: "Dressing in a grass skirt and donning a black face were seen as being demeaning. Large numbers of black organizations protested against the Zulu organization, and its membership dwindled to approximately sixteen men. James Russell, a long-time member, served as president in this period, and is credited with holding the organization together and slowly bringing Zulu back to the forefront."[2]

Said to be the first of New Orleans' Carnival krewes to integrate, the Zulus grew both in membership numbers and in parade size during the latter half of the twentieth century. By 2004, the parade included forty-seven floats, twenty-five marching bands, and fifteen drill units. After Hurricane Katrina, the number of floats dropped due to decreased membership and limited finances. In 2016, twenty-nine floats carrying 1,400 male and female maskers were interspersed with several bands and the popular Zulu Tramps and Zulu Walking Warriors marching units.

For many years, the Zulu parade rolled without any predetermined route, but snaked randomly through the streets of New Orleans' heavily African American neighborhoods, stopping at bars and other places of business to exchange toasts. Some years, the parade made it to the city's largest crowds on Canal Street, but without any regularity. In 1968, the city required Zulu to adopt and maintain a set route, which includes Jackson and St. Charles avenues, and Canal and Basin streets.

Each year since 1993, the Zulus have held their Lundi Gras Festival of music and merrymaking in the riverside Woldenburg Park. The next morning, Mardi Gras, the king and his retainers hit the streets at 8:30. Despite the relatively early hour of the parade and the excesses of many revelers during the previous night and days, the Zulu route is thickly lined by spectators determined to take in a spectacle not to be missed. The krewe holds a black-tie coronation ball the weekend before Mardi Gras that features a nationally famous singer or musical group. Tickets to the event can be purchased by the public.

3

Truck Parades and Superkrewes

With the advent of the automobile in the early 1900s, impromptu groups of maskers who had previously walked or ridden in animal-drawn conveyances began touring the New Orleans parade routes in motorized vehicles before, between, and after the parades. These revelers followed neither predetermined routes nor time slots but simply paraded the streets to see the sights and be seen in return. In 1935, Chris Valley organized a number of such costumed groups into the Krewe of Orleanians, which began the tradition of truck floats and formal truck parades.

Rather than the traditional parade floats built on specially designed chassis, the truck floats are huge everyday rigs with especially long beds decorated each year. Some of the truck floats are as elaborate in design as traditional floats, and their costumed riders toss great quantities of trinkets to the crowds. Truck floats often feature musicians, and the maskers aboard dance and sway in time to the beats.

The Orleanians follow the Rex parade on Shrove Tuesday. In 1973, they presented what was called the longest parade in the world, with a staggering number of 181 truck floats. Other popular truck parades are those of the Crescent City Carnival Club, founded in 1947, which follows the Orleanians; and the Krewe of Jefferson, founded in 1982, and the Elks Jeffersonians, established in 1984, both of whom follow the Krewe of Argus on Fat Tuesday in Metairie. Truck parades of yesteryear include those of the Krewe of St. Bernard Parish, which rolled in that parish from 1975 through 1985, and Elks Gretna, which paraded on the Westbank from 1983 through 2001. The popularity of the truck parades spread beyond Greater New Orleans and became a feature of Carnival celebrations in other parts of Louisiana, including Lafayette, Houma,

Morgan City, and Baton Rouge. The capital city is home to the heavily attended Spanish Town truck parade.

By the late twentieth century, the superkrewe parades of New Orleans Carnival came to attract the largest crowds of the season, featuring the most floats, the most marching bands, the most varied and numerous throws, celebrity monarchs, and world-famous guest riders. The prototypes for the superkrewes of today were Hermes and Babylon, both of whose parades continue to draw large turnouts and widespread acclaim.

Back in 1937, the Krewe of Hermes was founded in an effort to increase New Orleans tourism, which had declined with the financial distress of the Great Depression and the resultant shrinkage of the city's Carnival calendar to three major parades. King Hermes, who makes his appearance on the Friday night preceding Shrove Tuesday, wears a beard and makeup aboard his royal float, similar to Rex. Like the old-line krewe kings who don mysterious, full masks, though, Hermes remains anonymous to the public. The first queen of Hermes was Miss Marjorie Lee Smith in 1937. An innovative krewe, Hermes introduced neon lighting to its floats, though it still featured the traditional flambeaux. Hermes grew steadily through the years to include twenty-eight floats, fourteen bands, and many riding lieutenants.

The Knights of Babylon, who first paraded on the Wednesday night before Mardi Gras 1940, became famous for their electrically lighted floats, generous throws, and a lineup that grew to twenty floats by 2002. In 1992, Babylon switched its rolling time to Thursday night, a spot recently vacated by the Knights of Momus. Babylon's king is known as "Sargon," and his true identity is never made public. Sargon's first queen, in 1940, was Miss Julia Peytral.

Despite the excitement produced by the Hermes and Babylon parades, by the 1960s visitors' interest in Carnival appeared to be on the wane, with New Orleans hotels little more than half-full. In 1967, local advertising representative Ed Muniz filled the void on the Saturday night preceding Mardi Gras by spearheading the inaugural Krewe of Endymion parade. That first year, the men of Endymion rolled sixteen borrowed floats with the untraditional theme of "Take Me Out to the Ballgame." Also untraditional was Endymion's method of choosing its king by lots.

Two years later—in 1969—other New Orleans business and professional men paraded as the newly founded Krewe of Bacchus, with the theme "The Best Things in Life." With entertainer Danny Kaye as their first king, Bacchus established a precedent of celebrity kings that continues to form a highlight of the parade in the twenty-first century. Like their Endymion contemporaries, the men of Bacchus rode larger floats, such as the "Bacchasaurus," amid top-notch bands in longer parades, and threw huge amounts of trinkets to record-breaking crowds.

World-acclaimed singer Harry Connick Jr. and stage director Sonny Borey, both native New Orleanians, cofounded the superkrewe Orpheus, which first rolled on Lundi Gras night 1994. Orpheus' incredible "Leviathan" float, which breathes fire, was the first in the city's history to feature fiber-optic lighting.

Competition among the three superkrewes and smaller parading organizations resulted in some fantastic creations by New Orleans float builders Barth Brothers, Blaine Kern Artists, Cantrell & Son, Louis Masset, Royal Artists, Henri Schindler, and others. The "Pontchartrain Beach" float, which premiered in the Endymion parade of 2013, is 365 feet long, constructed on nine tandems by Blaine Kern Artists. Paying homage to the Zephyr roller coaster at the city's beloved Pontchartrain Beach amusement park, which closed in 1983, the float is capable of carrying nearly three hundred riders, more than the total membership of many an old-line krewe.

Increasingly, New Orleans has had to address the fluctuation between growth in the length of some krewe parades and shrinkage in others, as well as general safety concerns. In 2014, the city set the maximum number of parades at thirty, with a grandfather clause for those already in existence. Each parade is to have a minimum of fourteen floats and a maximum of forty-five "pull units" (that is, a float or tandem float drawn by tractor or mule power). The minimum number of marching bands required is seven for parades of 14 to 27 pull units, ten bands for parades of 28-36 pull units, and fourteen bands for the largest parades. Also in 2014, the growing tradition of many revelers roping off portions of streets, neutral grounds, and sidewalks for personal enjoyment as well as placing viewing ladders, tents, or cooking grills in these areas, was banned within six feet of a curb during parades by city ordinance. As part of their attempt to improve the quality of the parades, the New Orleans City Council ruled in 2003 that no single float should appear more than once on the downtown route during any single Carnival season.

Greater New Orleans'
Extensive Parade Calendar

Though the old-line parades and those of the superkrewes on the Uptown parade route continue to attract the most attention and largest crowds in the contiguous parishes of Orleans, Jefferson, and St. Bernard Parish, the area is home to dozens of other parades. By 2016, the parade calendar, as announced by *Arthur Hardy's Mardi Gras Guide* and the *Times-Picayune,* was as follows:

Twelfth Night: The Phunny Phorty Phellows, a krewe founded in 1981 and named in honor of a nineteenth-century organization of the same name, parades for early-season revelers from aboard the city's famous St. Charles Avenue streetcars. On the same night, which coincides with the birthday of St. Joan of Arc, the Krewe de Jeanne d'Arc, founded in 2010, holds its march through the French Quarter, led by an authentically costumed personification of the "Maid of Orléans" on horseback. The family-friendly krewe is active in year-round French cultural preservation causes.

Third Sunday preceding Shrove Tuesday: Li'l Rascals, a children's krewe dating from 1983 and named for the popular 1930s and 1940s films, parades in the afternoon in Metairie (Jefferson Parish) with nineteen floats.

Second Friday before Shrove Tuesday: Oshun, a primarily African American krewe with male and female members, founded in 1996, parades in downtown New Orleans at night with twenty floats. It is followed by Cleopatra, a women's krewe founded in 1972. Excalibur, a male and female krewe founded in 2002, rolls in Metairie at night aboard twenty-three floats. It is followed by Athena, a female krewe riding nineteen floats in its second annual parade.

Second Saturday before Shrove Tuesday: Adonis, founded in 1999, rolls at midday on the Westbank of the Mississippi River. Nemesis, a men's, women's, and children's krewe and St. Bernard Parish's only current Carnival parade, rides nineteen floats in the afternoon. On the Uptown route, the Krewe of Pontchartrain, founded in 1976 and originally rolling near Lake Pontchartrain, rides seventeen floats in the afternoon. Pontchartrain is followed by Choctaw, which first paraded in 1946 and is now a krewe of men, women, and children riding twenty-one floats. Choctaw is followed by Freret, organized in 2014 and bearing the name of an earlier krewe. The present parade features men and women riding fourteen floats. At night are Caesar, long famed for its elaborate costumes and feathered collars and headdresses, a men's krewe aboard twenty-five floats in Metairie; and on the Uptown route, two night parades—the Knights of Sparta, a male krewe that first rolled in 1982, aboard seventeen floats and featuring the first appearance of flambeaux on that route for the season, followed by Pygmalion, a male and female krewe organized in 2000, featuring seventeen floats.

Second Sunday before Shrove Tuesday: There are four parades in a row on the Uptown route, beginning in late morning. Femme Fatale, a women's krewe founded in 2015, makes merry aboard fifteen floats, followed by Carrollton, a men's krewe named for the neighborhood in which it was founded in 1924, presently rolling with twenty-six floats. Next comes King Arthur, established in 1977, with thirty-four floats bearing male and female krewe members, and finally Alla, an acronym for the Westbank town of Algiers, Louisiana, where the krewe was founded in 1933. Originally a men's krewe, Alla now has male and female members on twenty-four floats. At night, in Metairie, the co-ed krewe of Corps de Napoleon ride twenty-one floats replete with motifs and costumes reminiscent of Napoleon I.

Wednesday before Shrove Tuesday: There are two night parades on the Uptown route: the Ancient Druids, a male krewe founded in 1999, aboard twenty floats, followed by Nyx, a 2,200-plus-member female krewe founded in 2012, greeting fans from a lengthy parade of thirty-nine floats.

Thursday before Shrove Tuesday: There are three night parades on the Uptown route, starting with the Knights of Babylon, a twenty-three-float procession bearing male maskers and a secret king. Chaos follows, a sixteen-float procession using the chassis of the historic Momus parade and bearing a male krewe said to include Momus members since 2001. Finally comes the popular Muses parade of twenty-six floats, which also premiered in 2001. Female krewe members cast decorated high-heeled shoes and other specialty items to the crowds.

Friday before Mardi Gras, the greatest day for incoming air flights into New Orleans for the year: The first of three back-to-back night parades on the Uptown route is the visually stunning Hermes, with twenty-nine floats bearing the men's krewe and their anonymous king. Hermes is followed by the satirical male Krewe D'Etat, founded in 1998 and led by a secret ruler called the Dictator. This parade features twenty-four floats with flambeaux and float titles borne by shrouded men in the old-line tradition. Finally, there is Morpheus, god of sleep, appropriately, founded in 2002, with male and female members riding twenty-one floats. In Metairie, the male krewe of Centurions, founded in 1979, also rides twenty-one floats.

Saturday before Shrove Tuesday: A wide selection of parades begins in the morning on the Westbank, with the African American Krewe of NOMTOC, acronym for New Orleans Most Talked-Of Club, a male and female krewe established in 1971 and riding twenty floats. Uptown, beginning in late morning, is Iris, the city's oldest female krewe, which was founded in 1917, greeting admirers from thirty-seven floats. Iris is followed by Tucks, a forty-one-float parade with a male and female krewe, founded in 1969. Iris is famed for its comical features, such as a huge, rolling toilet bowl in which spectators are encouraged to toss trinkets caught from other floats. Late afternoon brings the superkrewe of Endymion with its thirty-six huge floats, king selected by lottery, celebrity grand marshal, guest riders, and membership of 3,100 males—the largest krewe in the city. In a dramatic parade conclusion, Endymion's floats enter the Mercedes-Benz Superdome, site of the post-parade ball. In Metairie, night is marked by the parade of Isis, founded in 1973, with eighteen floats bearing a female krewe.

Sunday before Shrove Tuesday: This day is popularly referred to since the mid-twentieth century as "Little Mardi Gras" for its full slate of parades and large crowds. Many of those attending prefer to come to-day rather than on Fat Tuesday itself. There are four parades, all on the Uptown route. Okeanos, which debuted in 1950 in the Ninth Ward, rolls in late morning with twenty relatively small, old-fashioned floats bearing a male cast, followed by the Krewe of Mid-City, named for the neighborhood in which it originated in 1934 and from which it rolled for many years. It processes with eighteen floats decorated in vivid tin-foil and bearing male and female maskers. Mid-City is followed by the thirty-seven floats of the large male Krewe of Thoth, founded in 1948 and nicknamed the "Krewe of Shut-Ins" as its route passes medical in-stitutions whose residents would have otherwise been unable to view a Carnival parade. Nighttime brings the spectacular Bacchus parade with its thirty-one superfloats bearing 1,400 male krewe members led by a celebrity king, followed by a post-parade ball held in the New Orleans Convention Center.

Monday before Shrove Tuesday: Lundi Gras features the meeting at the Mississippi riverfront of the gentlemen who will reign the next day as Rex and Zulu. At night are two parades on the Uptown route: the old-line Proteus krewe of 230 men and the Orpheus co-ed superkrewe. Proteus' secret king and his retainers ride twenty exquisitely detailed floats built on nineteenth-century chassis. The sight of the bejeweled and bearded Proteus, brandishing a glittering trident, from aboard his rocking throne set in a seashell drawn by seashores, all of realistic papier-mâché, has long been one of the most dramatic in American Carni-val history and the harbinger of Mardi Gras itself, only hours away. Directly behind, the superkrewe of Orpheus, founded in 1994, rides huge floats of modern but likewise striking artistry. At night in Metairie, the 200-member all-female Krewe of Pandora, in its Carnival premiere, greets the crowds from aboard sixteen floats, throwing specially decorated "Pandora's Boxes."

Mardi Gras: The great day itself begins early along the Uptown route: Zulu, the African king, and his 1,400 male and female retainers ride twenty-nine floats interspersed with some of the most talented and exuberant marching bands and dance units of the season. Following Zulu in midmorning is Rex, the King of Carnival, whose 455 male members greet the masses from aboard twenty-six floats of nineteenth-century inspiration but with themes considerably more recognizable for the majority of parade-goers. Truck parades follow Rex: the hundred units of the Elks Orleanians, founded in 1935 and the largest Carnival organization, with some 4,500 male and female riders of all ages, followed by the fifty-five trucks and 2,000 riders of the Crescent City Krewe, established in 1947. In Metairie, the Krewe of Argus, founded in 1972, parades in midmorning, with 600 men, women, and children aboard twenty floats, followed by the Elks Jeffersonians, established in 1975, with their truck parade of fifty-five units bearing 2,000 riders. The Elk Jeffersonians are followed by the Krewe of Jefferson truck parade, founded in 1973, and rolling with seventy-five units and 3,500 riders.

Throughout Shrove Tuesday—along the Uptown parade route, within the French Quarter, and in myriad neighborhoods of the city and its suburbs—appear the walking parades of established marching clubs as well as spontaneous maskers singly or in numbers. Those who never leave the French Quarter or their own neighborhoods need not join the crowds Uptown to participate in or simply view some of the passing show.

5

Erstwhile Parades

Between 1857 and 2014, more than sixty parading krewes were organized in the Greater New Orleans parishes of Orleans, Jefferson, and St. Bernard that have since been discontinued. The rise and fall of Carnival in the metropolitan area has been most noticeable in St. Bernard Parish, which once boasted more than a dozen krewes running per season and as many as five parades on Shrove Tuesday alone. Like many parades that continue today, several of the defunct krewes changed their rolling dates and routes through the years and/or combined with other krewes in an effort to remain on the street.

Lest their memory be limited to musty newspaper archives, the former parades of Greater New Orleans, their routes, and the years of their first and final appearances, are given here:

Adonis, Uptown, 1949–64.

Aladdin, Westbank, 2000–2005.

Alpheus, St. Bernard Parish, 1972–74.

America (designed for Fortune 500 riders), Uptown, Shrove Tuesday night, 1998–2000.

Amor, St. Bernard Parish, 1970–93.

Aphrodite, Uptown, 1962–64.

Aphrodite (a different krewe), St. Bernard Parish, 1986–2005.

Aquarius, St. Bernard Parish, 1975–76.

Aquila, Metairie, 1977–2008.

Arabi, St. Bernard Parish, long route through Ninth Ward to city center, 1957–86, and a single, last parade in 2005.

Ashanti (African American krewe), Uptown, 1993–96.

Ashanti-Vesta (successor to Ashanti), Uptown, a single parade in 1997.

Athena, Kenner, 1973–74.

Atlas, Metairie, 1969–2004.

Atreus, St. Bernard Parish, Shrove Tuesday, 1985–87.

Bards of Bohemia, Uptown, 1988–2005.

Bes, Westbank, 2008–9.

Camelot, Uptown, 1997–98.

Carnival, St. Bernard Parish, Shrove Tuesday, 1986–90.

Caronis, Uptown, a single parade in 1949.

Centaur, Kenner, a single parade in 1975.

Chalimar, St. Bernard Parish, 1976–80.

Comus, Uptown, Shrove Tuesday, 1857–1991.

Cronus, Westbank, 1953–65.

Cynthius (especially lavish parade by a male krewe), Uptown, 1947–51.

Daughters of Eve, St. Bernard Parish, 1973–79.

Diana, Metairie, 1969–99.

Druids, Uptown, Shrove Tuesday, 1922–34.

Freret, Uptown, 1953–93.

Freret-Pandora (successor to and combination of Freret and Pandora),
    Uptown, a single parade in 1994.

Gemini, Westbank, 1958–61.

Gladiators, St. Bernard Parish, 1974–2005.

Grela (acronym for Gretna, Louisiana, where it rolled), 1948–2015.

Haderus, St. Bernard Parish, a single parade in 1980.

Helios, Metairie, 1958–77.

Hercules, Gentilly, 1969–91.

Hesper, Kenner, 1972–74.

Hestia, Uptown, 1977–78.

Icarius, Uptown, 1982–85.

Independent Order of the Moon, Uptown, Shrove Tuesday, 1881–86.

Jason, Harahan, 1964–76.

Jason (a different krewe), 2004–7.

Jeffla (acronym for Jefferson, Louisiana), Westbank, 1949–51; merged with Midas in 1952.

Juno, St. Bernard Parish, 1970–82, combined with Jupiter, 1983–84; resumed and paraded as Juno, 1995–97.

Jupiter, St. Bernard Parish, 1969–82, combined with Juno, 1983–84.

Jupiter & Juno, combined krewes of Juno and Jupiter, St. Bernard Parish, 1983–84.

Love, Kenner, a single parade in 1982.

Marc Antony, Westbank, 1984–94.

Mardi Gras, founded as a parade comprised of floats from various krewes, Metairie, 1975–94.

Mecca, Uptown, 1968–78, merged twice: with Hestia as Hestia-Mecca and rolled 1979–80; with Sparta and paraded as Sparta-Mecca 1981–82. Mecca's doubloons were appropriately called "dinars."

Mercury, Metairie, 1986–2005.

Midas, Westbank, 1952–58.

Minerva, New Orleans East, 1977–92.

Mokana, Uptown, 1969–75.

Momus, Uptown, 1872–1991.

Nefertari, Westbank, 1975–95. The consort was called "Pharaoh," and the krewe threw unique hexagon-shaped doubloons.

Neptune, Metairie, 1996–97.

Nereus, single parade by this ball krewe in 1900, floats mounted on Uptown streetcars.

Nike, Westbank, single parade in 1974.

NOLAMISS (acronym for New Orleans, Louisiana, and Mississippi), children's krewe, 1972–75.

NOR (acronym for New Orleans Romance), Uptown, 1934–49, first children's parading krewe, rode miniature floats pulled by older children.

Octavia, Westbank, 1980–87.

Orion, Uptown, 1952–57.

Oz (children's krewe), 1981–84.

Palmares (Brazilian theme), Uptown, 1985–86.

Pan (children's krewe), St. Bernard Parish, 1972–78.

Pandora, New Orleans East, later Uptown, 1968–93; merged with Freret as Freret-Pandora, single parade in 1994.

Pegasus (especially plucky krewe that withstood cold and rainy weather and hurricane damage to floats), Uptown, 1966–2009.

Phoenix, Kenner, 1975–76.

Phunny Phorty Phellows, Uptown, Shrove Tuesday, 1878–85.

Poseidon, Westbank, 1959–2002.

Rhea, Metairie, 1971–2011.

Romulus & Remus, Kenner, single parade in 1973.

Samson & Delilah, St. Bernard Parish, 1983–85.

Saturn, Kenner and Metairie, 1983–2005.

Selena, New Orleans East, 1977–86.

Shangri-La, St. Bernard Parish, later Uptown, 1974–2008.

Silenus, Kenner, 1991–92.

Sinbad, Metairie, 1990–98.

Sprites (children's krewe), St. Bernard Parish, 1968–78.

Thebes (African American krewe), Uptown, single parade in 1995.

Thor, Metairie, 1973–2013.

Titans, St. Bernard Parish, 1983–84.

Ulysses, Westbank, 1989–2003.

Venus (first female parading krewe), Uptown, 1941–92.

Vikings of Tyr, St. Bernard Parish, 1972–75. King appropriately called "Odin."

Vulcan, Westbank, single parade in 1986.

Zeus, Metairie, 1958–2014.

Several of the above names are evident in the twenty-first-century Carnival calendar, including Phunny Phorty Phellows and Freret, but they are of newer organizations and have little if any relationship with these earlier krewes.

6

Walking Clubs and
Other Street Traditions

Though Carnival long existed primarily as a series of public parades and private balls coordinated by the men of New Orleans' social and financial elite, the more accessible Carnival "of the people"—staged by persons of average socioeconomic standing—has added its richness and diversity to the kaleidoscope of Mardi Gras merriment. The walking clubs, Mardi Gras Indians, alternative krewes, individuals masking, and many elements of French Quarter revelry now receive as much media attention as do the major parades.

A longstanding tradition of Carnival is the presence of the walking clubs, groups of citizens who costume according to a specific theme and march to music ahead of or among the lineup of the larger parades, or alone, apart from any parade. Members of these groups usually strut in time to the music—jazz or otherwise—and hand out artificial flowers in exchange for friendly kisses or hugs from spectators. The walking clubs that precede the Rex parade on Shrove Tuesday morning provide greatly anticipated and appreciated amusement for the massed thousands who await the coming of the King of Carnival.

The tradition of the walking club dates from the 1880s, and the oldest of these groups still marching today is the Jefferson City Buzzards, founded in 1890. In 1960, one of the most popular walking groups was founded by noted late New Orleans musician Pete Fountain. Pete Fountain's Half-Fast (double entendre intended) Walking Club is traditionally followed by the Mondo Kayo Social and Marching Club, just in front of the Zulu parade on Fat Tuesday. Having premiered in 1982, this Caribbean-themed group features a special commemorative doubloon each year.

One of the most popular walking clubs is the Society of St. Anne, a large assemblage of fantastically costumed men and women who begin their long Fat Tuesday march downriver and proceed into the bedlam of the French Quarter merrymaking. Dating from 1969, this group has become especially visible with increased media attention to the walking clubs in the wake of Hurricane Katrina. The Saint Cecilia marching organization, named for the patron saint of music, has paraded through the Faubourg Marigny on Shrove Tuesday each year since 2007. It is designed as a more neighborly promenade as opposed to the parades of the larger organizations on the more crowded routes of the city. Similarly, the St. Anthony Ramblers parade in Marigny and in the downriver part of the French Quarter on Mardi Gras morning. The Ramblers boast a "secret" route but usually meander from Mandeville Street to Jackson Square and beyond. Other walking clubs who have paraded through the years are the Garden District Club, Broadway Swells, St. Roch Carnival Club, Sons of Rest, Jan Jans, Vampy Vamps, Chrysanthemum Social Club, Lyons Club, Deep South Marching Club, Jefferson Royals, Sultans of Swing, Westbank Marching Club, Original West Side Carnival Club, Scene Boosters Social Aid & Social Club, Lady Buck Jumpers, Avenue Steppers Marching Club, and the Krewe of Grotesque and Outlandish Habiliments. The tradition of the walking clubs has spread beyond Greater New Orleans to Lafayette, Houma, Thibodaux, and Baton Rouge in the early twenty-first century. The Selucrey Sophisticats are among the most popular and regularly march in the Houma and Thibodaux parades.

A favorite event in the days leading up to Mardi Gras is the Krewe de Vieux parade, which rolls through parts of Faubourg Marigny, the French Quarter, and the Central Business District. Held on the third Saturday night before Mardi Gras, the parade consists of miniature, often risqué themed floats drawn by horses and flanked by costumed krewe members. Tracing its origins to an earlier group known as the Krewe of Clones, the Krewe de Vieux was founded in 1987. Like other organizations, Krewe de Vieux stages a ball after the parade. Following in the wake of Krewe de Vieux is the krewedelusion (note lowercase spelling) parade, an annual event since 2010. By 2016, some twenty sub-krewes were participating in this satirical parade of miniature floats and costumed characters. One of them, the Krewe de Jieux, has a membership of Jewish New Orleanians who march to jazz music with touches of the klezmer and hand out bagels and plastic "Jew eggs" that contain tiny yarmulke-clad dolls. In describing the 2013 showing, member Barbra Barnett stated that the krewe "uses anti-anti-Semitic comedy as its theme. Dressed up as bankers and media moguls, complete with plastic noses and blue horns, krewe members schlepped alongside a float that proclaimed a Jieux World Order. Think Borat, and then some."[1]

The second Saturday night before Mardi Gras is marked by the Intergalactic Krewe of Chewbacchus' sci-fi themed parade, which proceeds through the Ninth Ward, Faubourg Marigny, and French Quarter. In addition to maskers, the lineup consists of approximately one hundred rolling objects, including miniature floats, bicycles, and shopping carts, with the express exclusion of any "float" requiring internal combustion or petroleum products for movement. Members of the krewe, which premiered in 2011, make the signature soft throws and bead medallions.

One of the oldest Carnival traditions of the African American community of New Orleans is that of the Skull and Bones, dating back nearly two centuries and now staged in the Tremé section of the city, immediately to the "rear" of the French Quarter. For generations, maskers in relatively inexpensive, homemade skeleton costumes and similarly macabre accessories have paraded the area on Mardi Gras, beginning at sunrise, to represent the omnipresence of death and to frighten onlookers. In the twenty-first century, the North Side Skull and Bones organization continues the custom of what is one of the best manifestations of New Orleans' signature cultural response to mortality.

Widely recognizable and much anticipated during the annual Shrove Tuesday festivities are the Mardi Gras Indians. These marching groups costume as American Indians and parade the streets on Mardi Gras as well as on "Super Sunday," the Sunday closest to St. Joseph's Day (March 19). Possibly inspired by Buffalo Bill's Wild West Show, which was in New Orleans during Carnival 1885, New Orleanian Becaté Batiste founded the Creole Wild West marching club shortly thereafter. Through the years, innumerable similar organizations were formed, including the 101 Wild West, Apache Hunters, Black Eagles, Black Hawk Warriors, Creole Osceola, Flaming Arrows, Geronimo Hunters, Golden Arrows, Golden Blades, Golden Eagles, Golden Sioux, Mohawk Hunters, Morning Star Hunters, Original Yellow Jackets, Seminola Warriors, Seventh Ward Hunters, White Comanche Hunters, White Eagles, Wild Apache, Wild Bogocheetus, Wild Magnolias, Yellow Jackets, and Yellow Pocahontas.

The Mardi Gras Indians are territorial groups who usually follow no predetermined route but confine their activities to certain African American neighborhoods of New Orleans. Wearing magnificent costumes of robes, sequins, and feathers, they sing a number of chants dating from the early days of their history. An individual named Chief or Big Chief heads each Indian group. Other important offices are those of the Spy Boy, who keeps a lookout for "rival" tribes, and the Flag Boy, who relays messages to the Chief. Among many popular New Orleans songs reflecting the sociohistorical importance of the Mardi Gras Indians are "Big Chief," "Iko Iko," and "Jock-a-Mo."

At least two smaller Louisiana cities have featured Mardi Gras Indians in their pre-Lenten celebrations. In 1939 and 1940, the Houma print media noted young African American men and boys dressed as Indians on the parade route. In Lafayette, separate tribes of Mardi Gras Indians have a long tradition of strutting the streets on the big day, with many joining in the Lafayette Mardi Gras Festival parade in the afternoon.

Other noted maskers on foot who are part of New Orleans' African American tradition are the Baby Dolls: various groups of adult women dressed in frilly doll- or childlike dresses but dancing with gusto. This practice began in the heyday of Black Storyville, the city's red light district for African Americans during 1897–1917. Employees of brothels and dance halls thus attired took to the streets and "showed their linen" for the first time about 1910 and continued to do so for years as a competition to solicit male customers. In addition to wearing bloomers and bonnets, some of the early Baby Dolls smoked cigars and most carried whips or bricks as a form of protection from unwanted advances or dangers.

The public performance legacy of the Baby Dolls was carried on in black neighborhoods by residents who participated in groups such as the Gold Diggers, the Million Dollar Gold Diggers, and the Zigaboos. Their numbers peaked in the 1940s before the civil rights movement caused a reassessment of the dignity of the tradition and its historical ties with Black Storyville. The disruption of city life and tradition by Hurricane Katrina and the renaissance that followed was marked by renewed interest in the Baby Dolls' heritage.

Antoinette K-Doe founded a group in memory of her late husband, R&B singer and Pointe Coupee Parish native Ernie K-Doe (originally Cador), called the Ernie K-Doe Baby Dolls. In addition to advertising and branding the K-Doe business, the Mother-in-Law Lounge, the group is active in ministry to senior citizens and children, crafts, and fundraising. With the success of this group, approximately a half-dozen other Baby Doll groups had been formed by Mardi Gras 2016.

Street masking by the general public in the streets of the city on Shrove Tuesday is a tradition predating organized parades. Young and old, male and female, of various ethnicities, rich and poor—untold thousands have concealed their identity in fantastic costumes and masks and have celebrated with abandon since the earliest days of New Orleans Carnival. The range of character material for Mardi Gras costumes has ranged from no-cost old clothing from the attic trunk, to relatively inexpensive made-at-home creations, to the most elaborate and costly designs by professional costumers.

Costumes of the nineteenth century, described in contemporary newspaper accounts, included huge skirts that stretched from one side of the street to the other in the old French Quarter, huge papier-mâché heads, block-long "snakes" and "monsters" composed of interlinked individuals, plus disguises from the opulent to the beggarly and from the comical to the hideous. By the time of World War I, however, the most elaborate costumes had been forsaken for those of characters from the cinema, comic strips, the world of politics, and other common realms. One carryover from the old days, however, is a New Orleans ordinance that all masks are to be removed by sundown, a law promulgated in the rougher days of Carnival history when various nocturnal crimes are said to have been committed under the cover of masks.

Individual and group masking at Mardi Gras has declined through the twentieth and early twenty-first centuries, with changing tastes of the parade-going public. Those who continue to costume, however, still draw the admiration of plainclothes revelers for their creativity and the monetary expense that many of the most elaborate costumes require. Costume contests have long been a tradition in various parts of the city. Among the best known today are the exuberant contests staged by gay maskers in the French Quarter. The sightseer has much to witness in the elaborate, makeshift, coquettish, and risqué costumes sported by revelers in the Quarter and along the parade route.

As with other Carnival traditions, the allure of street masking by individuals and groups of revelers spread to smaller cities, including Lafayette, Houma, and New Roads. The tourist magazine *Louisiana Traveler* reported in 1957 that New Roads maskers celebrate "in the most rollicking manner" of any town outside the Crescent City. By the late twentieth century, the number of street maskers in these cities had dwindled drastically, but a few disguises may still be seen each season.

With the late twentieth-century shift in media interest from the pageantry and color of the grand Carnival parades to the inebriated abandon with which thousands celebrate in New Orleans, a common image has surfaced of drunken, drugged, and sexually provocative revelers clogging the streets and jamming the balconies of the French Quarter. Indeed many Americans, particularly young adults, make a pilgrimage to the Crescent City during Carnival—or for that matter, any time of the year—to behave as they would not normally in their hometowns. New Orleans' mainline Carnival community, city officials, and other concerned citizens have long denounced bawdy acts that have cast a poor light on the public image of American carnival as a whole. But each year, hundreds of revelers are arrested for improper behavior as New Orleans continues its mission to "clean up Carnival."

One of the most widespread lewd acts involves revelers baring their breasts and/or genitals in exchange for beads and other trinkets tossed down from French Quarter balconies or parade floats. As might be expected, Bourbon Street, with its numerous bars, lounges, and other places of entertainment dispensing liquor, is the center of this activity. In often frenzied attempts to reach the beads offered from above, some street-level revelers attempt to scale the metal columns or poles supporting the balconies. One of the street's most famed hostelries, the Royal Sonesta Hotel, has for years literally "greased the poles"—coating the first-floor columns with petroleum jelly—to prevent people from climbing. In true New Orleans fashion, this, too, has become a tradition and spurred an annual contest. Each year since 1970, the Royal Sonesta has hosted a popular "Greasing of the Poles" celebration in which locals and visiting celebrities attempt to climb the poles, to the delight of massed onlookers.

Whether they engage in promiscuous behavior or not, many thousands who visit New Orleans during Carnival never see a float, let alone an organized parade, but spend their entire stay in the French Quarter, taking in the sights and celebrating before the solemnity and abstinence of Lent. In 1979, for example, when a citywide police strike resulted in the cancellation of thirteen downtown parades and the movement of other krewes to suburban parade routes, an estimated 100,000 persons still jammed the French Quarter on Mardi Gras day. At midnight every Shrove Tuesday, mounted city police officers, many abreast on horseback, clear the streets of the French Quarter of the often bedraggled drunken revelers. Behind the police follows a fleet of motorized street cleaners, signifying the end of another New Orleans Carnival and a return to "normalcy" in the "City That Care Forgot."

7

Carnival Balls

The oldest Carnival tradition in New Orleans, dating from French colonial times, is that of the ball. Today, balls may be categorized as either "exclusive" or "public" events. Exclusive balls are those attended only by a krewe's carefully limited membership and invited guests, usually people within the krewe's social circle. Public balls, in contrast, are held by krewes that advertise for membership, and tickets are available to the general public. In almost all elite krewes, the identity of each year's king remains officially anonymous to the public. Newer krewes, however, usually make known the names of their kings and queens with much ado through pre-parade publicity. While it has been stated that the men of the old-line krewes "fight for the honor of anonymity," other men, and women, of the city proclaim their status as monarch for a day, or night, for the remainder of their lives.

The oldest krewes are the most exclusive regarding membership and invitations, and the members often introduce their daughters into society as debutantes. The most socially discriminating of the balls are those staged by the krewes of Comus, Momus, Proteus, Twelfth Night Revelers, and Atlanteans, all of which were established in the nineteenth century. Of the old-line krewes, Rex has historically been more generous in extending invitations beyond its immediate circle of intimates. Other old and elite ball krewes include those of the Mystic Club, Nereus, Olympians, Elves of Oberon, Osiris, Athenians, High Priests of Mithras, Prophets of Persia, Caliphs of Cairo, Moslem, Dorians, and Mystery. Among the newer krewes that stage fine balls are Eros, Harlequins, Squires, and the Children's Carnival.

Other krewes may imitate old-line customs of debutantes and invitation-only balls, but they are less stringent in their membership. The newer and larger superkrewes stage Carnival balls, complete with royalty, courts, and entertainment, but offer admission to the general public as well as to their own members and guests. Similarly, smaller neighborhood krewes open their balls and revelries to the public for an admission fee. Reflecting the names of their sponsoring organizations, some of these events include the Orpheuscapade, Bacchus Rendezvous, Endymion Extravaganza, Zulu Coronation Ball, Chewbacchus Chewbacchanal, Barkus Cocktail Pawty, Endymeow Bal Masque (with feline royalty), and Krewe of 'tit Rex Ping Pong Ball. The anti-establishment Krewe du Vieux and gay Krewe de Satyricon balls are also open to the public for admission.

The old-line balls, whether staged by parading or non-parading krewes, continue to form one of the highlights and most revered traditions of Carnival in New Orleans. From Twelfth Night (January 6), or even before, to Shrove Tuesday night, the various circles of New Orleans society celebrate with elaborate tableaux, dancing, and the presentation of debutantes to make-believe royalty amid "courts" of brilliant scenery and ceremonials. The 1947 observations of Robert Tallant in *Mardi Gras* hold true in the twenty-first century:

> Orleanians await the receipt of invitations to balls with feverish anxiety. It is quite true that there are people who loathe balls, but no one, especially the female portion of the population, will admit it, for by the number of invitations received do many of them measure their popularity, and by the quality of the balls to which they are asked may be judged their social position (14). . . .
>
> For all the weeks between Twelfth Night and Mardi Gras, New Orleans blazes with lights and jewels, brilliant costumes and dazzling evening gowns and the dignity of white ties and tails, as the balls go on night after night. There are a few individuals, usually male, who tire of it all, but for most Orleanians and their visiting friends it all accumulates into the biggest show on earth, for where else in the

world is there left such concentration upon the spectacular? Where else can one move from court to court, from land to land, to be welcomed each night by different royalty in an entirely different setting? Where else can one perhaps become royalty, even if only for a single night? Where else can one completely escape into another world and another age? In most Americans there lurks an atavistic affection for monarchy (27).

At most formal balls, the old Carnival favorite "If Ever I Cease to Love," the grand march from *Aida,* or another stately selection is played by an orchestra as the royalty and their attendants circle the ballroom floor in the grand march, and their make-believe majesties are acclaimed by the audience as if the couples were true royalty indeed. The subsequent presentation of debutantes to the enthroned kings and queens is the eagerly anticipated "coming out" event for countless young New Orleans women. Like parades, balls are designed and executed according to a specific theme each year, and following the grand march and presentations, costumed krewe members act in tableaux, or scenes revealing episodes or aspects of the chosen themes. Krewes that parade and hold balls have identical themes for each.

Oral tradition of several generations told of one New Orleans gentleman who reigned over a record number of four krewes in a single Carnival season, specifically in a week's time. In 2014, Arthur Hardy's annual *Mardi Gras Guide* revealed his identity as Dr. Paul Gelpi. The young physician accepted the successive invitations to rule over the krewes of Atlanteans, Momus, Proteus, and Comus in 1904. He was supposedly invited by the Rex organization to rule as King of Carnival that same year but, as he had already accepted Comus' honors, he logically had to decline those of Rex, owing to the two monarchs' traditional meeting on Mardi Gras night and his inability, therefore, "to meet himself."

Dr. Gelpi's niece, Miss Gladys Gelpi, was the most feted of New Orleans Carnival debutantes, reigning twice as queen and serving as maid in six courts in the year 1931. The *Times-Picayune* social columns for the first two months of that year name Miss Gelpi scores of times in recounting her presence at dinners, dances, and other functions of the season. She was successively a maid in the courts of Nereus, Osiris, Athenians, Mithras, Mystery, and Momus; Queen of Proteus; and, finally, Queen of Carnival, as Rex's consort.

The annual selection of queens and attendant maids from college-age debutantes provides for much anticipation among New Orleans krewe families until the official announcements are made at or soon after New Year's. The Twelfth Night Revelers retain the lovely tradition of rolling a huge imitation cake into the ballroom and distributing its "slices"—small cardboard boxes—to pre-chosen debutantes. Those who receive a silver bean within their slices are named maids of the court, while the lucky recipient of the single golden bean is crowned queen, the entire presentation and distribution being carefully prearranged. Miss Emma Butler was the first queen to reign over Twelfth Night, in 1871.

Throughout the history of Carnival in New Orleans, a number of public facilities have served as venues for the balls, the most famous of which was the elegant French Opera House that stood on Bourbon Street from 1859 until it burned down in 1919. Various other sites served the ball krewes until the opening of the ten-thousand-seat New Orleans Municipal Auditorium, just outside of the French Quarter, in 1930. There, most of the balls were held until the close of the twentieth century when the facility was turned into a gambling casino. The auditorium opened its doors to the elegant balls once more for a brief period between the closing of the casino and Hurricane Katrina. It has yet to reopen.

The visitor to the city, along with much of the New Orleans population, has little chance of attending exclusive balls because each krewe member is allotted only a few invitations and these go, invariably, to family members and intimate friends. The krewes are tight-knit groups, not unlike extended families, especially those dating from the 1800s. Generations ago, Atlanteans acquired the reputation as the most select of the ball krewes, extending very few invitations outside their membership. A long-time quip has been about whom one "did not see" (that is, had failed to be invited) rather than whom one "did see" (most of society) at any given Atlanteans ball.

Guests to the exclusive balls, unlike the krewe members and royalty, do not costume, but wear full evening dress: white tie and tails for men, floor-length gowns for women. Presidents, ambassadors, royalty, and military heroes have been among the honored guests at the city's Carnival balls through the generations. Undoubtedly the most celebrated visitors were the Duke of Windsor, formerly King Edward VIII of Great Britain, and his duchess, who attended the Rex Ball of 1950. After much public speculation and anticipation, the former king and his consort bowed like the rest of the ball-goers to the make-believe New Orleans royalty, and the event is considered one of the prime points in New Orleans and Carnival history.

In the old-line krewes and some founded subsequently, select female invitees of the balls receive coveted "call out" cards signifying that certain of the masked members of the male krewes will call out and dance with them. In the case of female krewes, the pattern is reversed, with the maskers calling out male guests to dance. At the end of each dance, the participating krewe members present "favors," or souvenirs, to the guests they have called out to dance. These favors, which range from inexpensive ornaments to costly, jeweled items, often are marked with the name of the krewe and year of the ball. Ball favors rank along with old invitations, early vintage doubloons, and nineteenth- and early twentieth-century lithographed prints of the parade floats as some of the most sought-after collectible items of American Carnival. By the end of the twentieth century, some New Orleans krewes discontinued the tradition of call-out, tableaux balls and have opted instead for rollicking supper dances with gourmet dining and animated dancing.

Though most of New Orleans' traditional Carnival balls have been hosted by krewes with predominantly white, old-line family and social membership, other communities adapted the custom to their own preferences. In the African American community, a number of balls staged more or less in the manner of the white krewes have been held for generations by respected organizations, including the Young Men Illinois and the Original Illinois. These elaborate events are orchestrated according to themes reflecting literary or mythological subjects and provide select opportunities for debutantes to be presented as well as for dancing and socializing. Miss Emma Fortier, the first known debutante to be thus honored, reigned over the Original Illinois inaugural ball in 1895. Combining elements of old and new, the Zulu organization stages a ball each year, four days prior to its parade.

During the nineteenth and much of the twentieth century, New Orleans' numerically and culturally significant Jewish culture was largely excluded from old-line Carnival events, including membership in krewes and attendance at balls. Superficially, relations remained amiable during Carnival time between prominent Gentiles in the krewes and their Jewish business partners and acquaintances. The Harmony Club, a Jewish fraternal and social organization with a beautiful clubhouse at the corner of St. Charles and Jackson avenues, hosted its own Carnival ball for some years. The club also had the custom of assembling on the street with champagne and toasting Rex as the king and his krewe passed. One year shortly before World War I, however, Rex did not pause before the club, the Harmony Club was not acknowledged, and no toast was exchanged. Generations of Jewish New Orleanians remembered the incident, and many chose to conveniently be out of the city during Carnival. Interest in the Harmony Club ball waned among its members and potential guests, and that tradition was ended as well.

New Orleans has long been a center of gay culture, though many years of prejudice against the lifestyle from the mainstream of society prevented much of gay events from being documented on an appreciable scale. Early events such as Carnival balls within this segment of the population were held in homes and other inconspicuous places until a more accepting attitude by the general public allowed gay events to be held in larger and more visible public facilities. Even in their early, mostly invisible years, the gay Carnival balls of New Orleans were known for their extravagant costumes, choreography, and settings.

The oldest known gay krewe is Yuga, which was founded in 1959 and presented its first ball in 1962. Subsequently formed krewes include Petronius, Armeinius, the Celestial Knights, Krewe of David, Polyphemus, Satyricon, Dasimé, Lords of Leather, Dirty Dottie, Ganymede, Ishtar, Memphis, MKA, Olympus, Perseus, Phoenix, Satin & Sequins, Vista, and Amon-Ra. Despite prevailing attitudes in the early days, many women from mainstream New Orleans society solicited invitations from and attended these krewes' events. With more accepting attitudes from the general public and the organizations' subsequent move to larger public venues, attendance at the balls increased. The St. Bernard Cultural Center in suburban Chalmette was the scene of most gay Carnival balls in the 1970s and 1980s, after which the majority moved to the Municipal Auditorium in New Orleans.

One of the latest official tallies of the total number of Carnival balls in New Orleans, made by Arthur Hardy for the 2002 season, stood at seventy-one. Changing tastes among krewes and their potential guests, the relatively high cost of staging elaborate tableaux balls, and rents charged by public facilities have been cited as prime reasons for the decline in the number of balls during the late twentieth and early twenty-first centuries. Many ball krewes have been discontinued, and among some that have survived, the ball format has changed to dinner dances or similar, less formal events. Some of the ball krewes that have come and gone are Grand Duke Alexis, Les Mysterieuses, the Mittens, Aglaia, the Terpsichorean Revelers, Mystic Maids, Artemisians, Promethians, Yami, Les Innconnues, Argonauts, Amphyctions, Titanians, Empyreans, Votaries of Indra, Arcadians, Nippon, Consus, Falstaffians, Les Ecoliers, the Knights of Folly, Alexandrians, Butterflies, Carnival Clowns, Hesperides, the Knights of Ransom, Follies, Carnival Revelers, Iridis, and Caputanians.

The annual meeting of the courts of Comus and Rex, the traditional finale of the Carnival season and Mardi Gras on Shrove Tuesday night, was televised annually from 1953 until 1991. With the New Orleans City Council's passage of anti-discrimination legislation as regards Carnival organizations in 1991, however, Comus discontinued televising the ritual for several seasons. Coverage resumed with the dawn of the twenty-first century, and the meeting officially closes the Carnival season for many television viewers.

The elegance, romance, and cultural diversity of New Orleans' Carnival balls proved infectious to krewes in smaller Louisiana cities, many of which have staged their own tableaux and debutante balls for generations. Among those cities and towns staging exceptional Carnival balls—by parading and non-parading krewes—are Baton Rouge, Lafayette, Houma, Thibodaux, Franklin, Morgan City, Plaquemine, St. Martinville, Opelousas, and New Roads.

8

Carnival Food and Drink

In a city noted worldwide for its distinctive as well as wide range of cuisine, Carnival is a season of special culinary and spirituous celebration for residents and visitors alike. The perennial merriment begins for many on January 6 with the partaking of king cake (*gâteau du Roi*). A circular confection made of brioche dough, usually glazed in icing and purple, gold, and green sugar, the king cake may have one or more of a wide range of fillings and normally contains a tiny plastic baby or other trinket. Whoever receives the baby or trinket in their slice of cake is usually expected to provide the king cake on the next occasion. The tradition carries on through Fat Tuesday.

Louisiana has at least one annual festival for nearly every one of its signature foods, and king cake is no exception. Early in the Carnival season, Ochsner Health System hosts a king cake festival. Held at the Mercedes-Benz Superdome to benefit infants and children at Ochsner's children's hospital, the event includes a king cake bake-off by competitive bakeries, fitness challenge exercises, a marathon fun run, and a slate of musical performances.

Within the secret sanctums of Carnival krewes and their royalty, elaborate brunches, luncheons, and dinners are served for members and select guests. Cocktail parties and other soirees held in the homes of royal and debutante families before and after the balls and parades likewise provide for banqueting and toasting. Many homeowners along the parade routes host an open house for family and friends. Indoor buffets and outdoor barbecues and crawfish boils are typical offerings.

Alcohol, imbibed in great quantity in the city 365 days and nights a year, flows freely during Carnival. Women were once barred all days

of the year but Mardi Gras from entering and drinking at the famed
Sazerac Bar. Today, most bars and lounges have no restrictions on entry
or on the purchase of alcohol by any customer of legal age. And conveniently for parade-goers, New Orleans permits drinking alcoholic bev-
erages in open plastic containers (but no glass) on the street.

SOURCES FOR PART I: *Daily Picayune,* New Orleans; *The Item,* New Orleans; *Times-
Picayune,* New Orleans; *Louisiana Weekly,* New Orleans; *State-Times,* Baton Rouge; *Louisiana Traveler,* 1957; LaCour, *New Orleans Masquerade*; Perry Young, *The Mystick Krewe:
Chronicles of Comus and His Kin* (New Orleans: Carnival Press, 1931); Charles L. Dufour
and Leonard V. Huber, *If Ever I Cease to Love: One Hundred Years of Rex, 1872–1971* (New
Orleans: School of Design, 1970); Hardy, *Mardi Gras Guide;* www.mardigras.com; www
.zulu.com/history; joanofarcparade.org; kingcakefestival.org; louisiana.kitchenandculture
.com/louisiana-mardi-gras-parade-schedule.

PART II

ACADIANA

Southwest Louisiana includes most of the state's French Triangle, home to the greatest number of descendants of the Acadian French, who were systematically exiled from their native Nova Scotia by British overlords beginning in 1755. Settling among earlier Creole French, German, African American, and Native American populations, the Acadians and their descendants, commonly called *'Cadiens* or *Cajuns,* introduced the Courir de Mardi Gras (Running Mardi Gras) tradition in the 1780s. The growth of towns, the influx of Anglo-Americans, and an increased knowledge of New Orleans' Carnival parades and balls resulted in the formation of formal parades of floats and bands in some Acadiana parishes in the late nineteenth and early twentieth centuries.

9

Courir de Mardi Gras

I n 1941, Harnett T. Kane wrote in his popular book *The Bayous of Louisiana:*

> The world has heard much of the New Orleans Mardi Gras, with its tall floats of papier-mâché, kings riding high above the populace, and costume balls and tableaux. For generations the prairies have had their rural version, and in one instance, as I know, at least as much fun.
>
> "Courir Mardi Gras" . . . is the name of the observance. This Fat Tuesday is almost a race, and a daylong one. A thing primarily for men and horses, it consists of impromptu hell-raising that had no place for the girls; no queens on balconies, no costume ball with court of honor, although there is a happy fais-do-do (dance) in the evening.[1]

City and town dwellers have long been fascinated with this "other" or "country" Mardi Gras. An annual custom said to date from as early as the 1780s, the traditional *courirs* consist of costumed men, numbering from a few to 2,000 or 3,000, led by a *capitaine* riding from house to house on Mardi Gras morning, singing traditional French songs and procuring ingredients for a community gumbo. The costumes worn by the courir riders range from the hilarious to the hideous, with men often disguised as women. There are all types of masks, including the hand-fashioned wire-mesh variety that has been a custom in many communities for several generations. Among the traditional types of hats are the *capuchon,* a dunce-like hat resembling the peaked hats of the medieval age; the mortarboard model, which mocks scholarly matters; and a mitre form that pokes fun at the religious hierarchy.

Best known of these countryside celebrations is the one held around Mamou in Evangeline Parish. The Mamou courir tradition began in antebellum times and continued until a shooting marred the 1940 celebration. After a twelve-year lapse, the custom was revived in 1953, and in recent years it has become an increasingly popular tourist attraction. Visitors need not worry about arriving late for the festivities, as it is a daybreak-to-midnight celebration. Local landmark Fred's Lounge is a mecca for tourists, with many imbibing at an extremely early hour on the big day.

As many as 20,000 revelers have been estimated by police officials to crowd Mamou on Fat Tuesday to greet the riders, and 30,000–35,000 for the extended Mardi Gras weekend. Exceptions were the chilly and damp Shrove Tuesday of 2004, when attendance was numbered at 9,000, and the freezing rain of 2014, when mere hundreds braved the elements as dozens of riders bundled up and made the best of it. Year after year, as regional television brings scenes of the Mamou courir to its viewers, members of the colorful courir band boast on-camera: "This is the real Mardi Gras!"

The courir at Basile, another Evangeline Parish community, also has early origins, though it was suspended during World War II. Revived in the 1960s, the celebration lasts eight to nine hours. Though it was staged on horseback prior to World War II, the Basile run is now carried out on large trucks. Since the early 1980s, women have participated as well as men. The maskers are called *sauvages* (savages) and act with mock terrorism toward spectators, in addition to begging for ingredients for the gumbo.

For spectators unable to attend the Basile courir, the performers stage a run on an earlier date at the Vermilionville interpretive center just outside the city of Lafayette. Riders stop and beg for gumbo ingredients at six of the period homes that formerly stood at various locations in Acadiana. Events begin with a children's capuchon-making workshop. Following the run are a children's chicken chase for prizes, the serving of the gumbo, and music and dancing at the Bal du Dimanche (Sunday Dance).

Trucks have also carried the participants of the courir at Tee Mamou (*tee* is short for *petit,* or small) near Iota in Acadia Parish ever since the frigid 1919 Mardi Gras when two-thirds of the twenty-eight horses employed that year died of pneumonia after the run. The Tee Mamou celebration, which dates from at least the early 1900s, has been part of a larger Tee Mamou–Iota Mardi Gras Folklore Festival since 1988 and usually attracts an estimated 8,000–10,000 onlookers. When the riders return to town, they chant traditional Carnival songs dating back four centuries, dance with available females, and beg for loose change. A separate women's run opens the Tee Mamou–Iota festivities on the Saturday of Mardi Gras weekend.

The courir at l'Anse de 'Prien Noir, near Duralde in Evangeline Parish, is not as well known to the outside world. Many of its participants descend from the Cyprien "'Prien Noir" Cézaire namesake and other early settlers of the area. The Creole music made famous by later residents Amedée Ardoin and cousin Alphonse "Bois Sec" Ardoin is as much a part of today's festivities as it was one hundred years ago.

Eunice, in St. Landry Parish, began its tradition of Courir de Mardi Gras in 1920 but allowed it to lapse. This custom was revived in 1946 and is a popular event today. A courir for children has been held on the Sunday before Mardi Gras since 1991, and is followed by a traditional *boucherie* (hog butchering), cookout, and feasting. The principal, adult run is held on Mardi Gras day. Throughout the extended weekend and Shrove Tuesday, interpretive programs describing the rural Mardi Gras traditions are held at the Prairie Acadian Cultural Center in Eunice. Jam sessions at Liberty Theatre and street dancing keep the Carnival spirit going for days.

The number of riders in Eunice's courirs rose dramatically to approximately 2,500 for the adult event and about 600 for the children's run by 2002, according to city officials. Just six years earlier, in 1996, the adult ride had numbered but 484 riders. As regards spectators, some 15,000 were anticipated for Mardi Gras 2014, but mercury in the twenties and freezing rain kept attendance to the hundreds.

Church Point, in Acadia Parish, holds two popular courirs on the weekend prior to Mardi Gras: an adult run, established in 1962, on Sunday, and an alcohol-free and horseless children's run on Saturday, founded in 2002. By the early twenty-first century, the Church Point men's courir, stretched with forty floats and wagons in addition to horsemen. The Saturday morning before Mardi Gras is also marked by runs in Elton, in Jefferson Davis Parish, and at the Horse Farm of the Lafayette Farmers Market. The latter, inaugurated in 2014, includes a children's chicken chase, followed by live music.

In recent decades, increased media coverage has brought attention to courirs held in other localities, such as the following:

Acadia Parish
Egan
Lejeune Cove

Calcasieu Parish
Iowa

Evangeline Parish
L'Anse aux Pailles, Chataignier
Pine Prairie
Turkey Creek

Iberia Parish
New Iberia

Jefferson Davis Parish
Lake Arthur

St. Landry Parish
Cankton
Grand Prairie
L'Anse Maigre
Lawtell
Pecaniere
Port Barre

In many of these processions, other maskers ride on improvised floats and in wagons and trucks in addition to the usual lines of costumed horsemen. Some runs are largely held by and for extended family and friends on the weekend before Mardi Gras. It is impossible to know when and where every courir is staged, and local residents as well as visitors may happen upon one by chance when driving the rural byways of southwest Louisiana during the season.

10

Lafayette and Environs

While New Orleans and Mobile continue their debate over which has the older pre-Lenten celebration, Lafayette, the hub of Acadian French Louisiana, boasts of the second-largest Mardi Gras attendance in the nation. Though surrounded by the rustic, rural Courir de Mardi Gras celebrations, Lafayette, as principal city of the region, developed an urban version of Carnival festivities, along the line of New Orleans' parades and balls. Nine parades have constituted Lafayette's Carnival calendar since 2006, and the number of spectators who attend the five-day, Friday–Tuesday events have been estimated at a total of 500,000 by parade and law enforcement officials.

History

In their 1957 book *Allons à L'Acadie,* Frances and John Love colorfully described Mardi Gras in mid-twentieth-century Lafayette:

> Gorillas, chain gangs, pirates, gypsies, hoop-skirted belles, and overgrown rabbits cavort through the crowds kicking beer cans and calling to recognizable friends. A parade comes by every few hours. Children shout to men atop floats to throw them a favor.
>
> Anyone who reaches into the air catches a string of beads, a black rubber spider, or a silver tin whistle.
>
> King Gabriel toasts Queen Evangeline from his float throne in mid-town during the morning parade. In the afternoon the king of the colored folk parades by. Just before dark Queen Evangeline's parade takes place. It is a rare Mardi Gras day that does not get a rain

or two. But nothing dampens the spirits of the revelers. Lent begins with an epidemic of colds, sinus infections, and hangovers. (13)

By the time the above was written, Lafayette's Mardi Gras was already a longstanding tradition. The city's earliest recorded Carnival ball is said to have occurred in 1869. Three decades later, in 1897, Lafayette's first known parade rolled. King Attakapas, whose name honors the great Indian tribe of South Louisiana, headed a seven-float parade, with his dukes representing the smaller towns of Lafayette Parish. Serving as King Attakapas was George Armand Martin while Miss Isaure McDaniel reigned as his queen.

The twentieth century saw the establishment of numerous ball krewes, among them Oberon, in 1929; Gabriel, 1949; Troubadours, 1952; Les Brigands de Lafitte, 1954; Lafayette Mardi Gras Association, 1958; Attakapas, 1968; Versailles, 1975; Bonaparte, 1976; Apollo, 1979; Triton, 1979; Augustus, 1983; Camelot, 1984; D'Argent, 1986; Olympus, 1988; Xanadu, 1990; Victoria, 1993; Renaissance, 1995; Jeunes Amis, 1997; and Celts, 1998. Most of these krewes continue to stage elaborate court presentations and tableaux in the fashion of old New Orleans Carnival.

The public celebration of Fat Tuesday has been an annual tradition in Lafayette since 1934, with the early parades staged by the Southwest Louisiana Mardi Gras Association. This umbrella organization was founded in 1933 specifically to promote and organize parades in the area. Lafayette's parading tradition is, therefore, the state's third oldest, following New Orleans and New Roads. From 1934 on, King Gabriel and Queen Evangeline have reigned over the Lafayette festivities, their titles honoring the hero and heroine of Longfellow's epic poem "Evangeline." Reigning as the first Gabriel and Evangeline were George Gardiner and Miss Mable Broussard. For many years, Lafayette's Carnival celebration was limited to Shrove Tuesday, with Gabriel—who through 1961 arrived in the city by train for the occasion—parading with his krewemen in the morning, a children's parade of mini-floats in the afternoon, and an illuminated night parade. Queen Evangeline first led the Mardi Gras night parade in 1965, but she and the parade moved to Lundi Gras night in 1970.

The earliest parade floats in Lafayette were mule drawn, and those of the night parades were illuminated by flambeaux. Another aspect of the early years was a longstanding municipal ordinance prohibiting complete costuming by the street masses: persons who wore masks were required to leave their hands bare, which may have been a way to distinguish white from African American revelers in the days of racial segregation. Erstwhile Lafayette parades include the Quota parade, a Saturday afternoon event begun in 1947 and discontinued by 1958; the Court of Diotima women's parade, which rolled only once, on Mardi Gras afternoon in 1953; and the Krewe of Triton, which likewise held but a single parade, directly behind the Queen's parade of 2000.

Carnival festivities in Lafayette were suspended from 1942 to 1947 because of World War II and in 1951 during the Korean conflict. In all other years, however, the parades continued, oftentimes in spite of uncompromising weather. The 1978 Fat Tuesday parades rolled in sleet. Lafayette's record-worst Shrove Tuesday weather occurred in 2014, with the temperature in the low thirties and a freezing drizzle during King Gabriel's parade and that of the Lafayette Mardi Gras Association. All marching bands canceled except one in each parade. By the time the Independent parade began, the mercury had risen just above freezing and the precipitation changed to rain as less than the usual number of floats rolled. Though attendance in 2013 consisted of crowds lined two to more than four rows deep along the parade route, the 2014 turnout consisted of sporadic clusters of shivering and wet onlookers.

The Fat Tuesday crowd in Lafayette was estimated by local newspapers at 40,000 in 1941 and grew to 100,000 by 1955. Published attendance estimates usually ranged from 100,000 to 150,000 during the 1970s and 1980s and rapidly increased thereafter. Exceptions were the bitterly cold celebrations of 1978, when the crowd was numbered at 40,000–50,000, and 1989, when it was estimated at 60,000–70,000. By 2006, local police officials estimated that 250,000 persons normally viewed each of the individual parades. The Lafayette parade route—like those of New Orleans and other cities—is protected by an extensive system of barricades, and law enforcement officers work to limit excessive alcohol consumption and brawls. Lengthening of Lafayette's parade route in the latter decades of the twentieth century reduced the crowding of spectators and associated jostling for throws.

Lafayette Parade Calendar

The night of the second Saturday preceding Mardi Gras is marked by the Krewe of Carnivale en Rio parade. It premiered in 2006 with twenty-two Brazilian-inspired floats and six bands and grew to include twenty-five floats bearing 650 riders, plus cyclists and other performers in 2016.

Since 1999, the second Sunday before Fat Tuesday has been marked in Lafayette by a dog parade, the Krewe des Chiens, which premiered with about 100 costumed dogs led by their owners before some 200 spectators. Within just a few years, the event had grown to feature 120 dogs and an attendance estimated at 20,000 by city police officials.

The Krewe of Roux parade rolls on the Thursday afternoon preceding Mardi Gras. Founded in 1998, this parade was established by and for the students of the University of Southwestern Louisiana—now the University of Louisiana at Lafayette—and proceeds through the campus.

Named for the night on which it rolls, the Friday Night Kickoff parade premiered in 1998 with seventeen floats and seven bands. Sponsored by the Southwest Louisiana Mardi Gras Association, this parade—like the Queen's and children's parades—features riders from various Lafayette krewes. This parade has been a relatively fast grower, with the 2005 lineup having fourteen marching bands among the floats. Of the twenty-three floats that rolled in 2014, one was destroyed and all others damaged on the following morning by a severe wind, rain, and hail storm. All were quickly repaired in order to be used for the Krewe of Bonaparte parade.

Children's Carnival festivities have long been a tradition in Lafayette. With the establishment of the Southwest Louisiana Mardi Gras Association, a juvenile Mardi Gras afternoon parade was born. After an absence of several years, the children's parade resumed and by 1979 switched its rolling time to the Saturday afternoon preceding Fat Tuesday. Participants include the Krewe of Oberon, founded in 1928, and other area children's krewes. Growing through the years, the colorful children's parade lineup stretched with as many as nineteen floats and ten bands in the early twenty-first century. Published attendance estimates of the annual event rose as high as 100,000.

The Krewe of Bonaparte parade had its origins in 1972 as a part of Queen Evangeline's Monday night parade. In 1986, however, Bonaparte became a separate parade, marching on the Saturday night preceding Mardi Gras. The fun-loving krewe has since delighted the public with as many as twenty-four illuminated floats and a large number of top-notch marching bands.

The Sunday afternoon preceding Mardi Gras is marked by two parades just outside Lafayette: the Krewe des Amis in Youngsville and the Krewe of Karencro in Carencro. Approximately eighty units participated in the 2014 Youngsville parade, which was viewed by hundreds of spectators. The Karencro parade, which premiered in 1981 and is led each year by King Louis and Queen Anna, attracts 20,000–30,000 spectators along its three-and-a-half-mile route, according to organizers.

Queen Evangeline, who originally rolled on Mardi Gras night, has paraded on Lundi Gras night since 1971. Float riders represent a number of Lafayette krewes. Icy, subfreezing weather spurred the cancellation of the Queen's parade in 1989. Having first rolled with twelve floats, Queen Evangeline's parade grew to include as many as twenty-two illuminated floats by the late 1990s. At that point, the Southwest Louisiana Mardi Gras Association shortened the Queen's parade to twelve floats and created a whole new Friday night parade. By 2002, however, the number of floats in the Queen's parade had again risen to seventeen. The marching bands in this parade, anywhere from seven to fifteen each year, have consistently proven a top attraction.

King Gabriel's first parade rolled with six floats and grew to include twelve floats and twenty bands by 1965. Now featuring seventeen huge, New Orleans–built floats and from five to ten marching bands, Gabriel follows an east-west path through Acadiana's hub city each Fat Tuesday morning. The route has been lengthened and modified through the years, and by 2016 stretched for four miles.

Lafayette's African American community held its first known Fat Tuesday parade on Mardi Gras afternoon 1950 when King Balthazar and Queen Mezzo led the Lafayette Carnival Club for Colored People. Since 1959, the community has enjoyed the Lafayette Mardi Gras Festival parade, which features fifteen to seventeen floats interspersed, in recent years, with from five to eleven lively marching bands. Reigning monarchs are dubbed "King Toussaint l'Ouverture," after the hero of Haitian independence, and his consort, Queen Suzanne Simonne. Joining the lineup are Lafayette's Mardi Gras Indians, who parade through individual neighborhoods in the morning and file into the line of floats and bands in the afternoon.

The third and final parade on Fat Tuesday in Lafayette is the Independent parade, a procession open to public participation and usually consisting of approximately thirty truck floats. Since 1993, the Southwest Louisiana Mardi Gras Association has coordinated Le Festival de Mardi Gras à Lafayette, held at Cajun Field on Friday through Tuesday of Mardi Gras weekend. This is the disbanding point of the parades, where food, music, and midway rides are offered in a family-friendly setting.

Several civic-type Carnival parades—that is, parades open to public participation rather than staged by private krewes—were organized in towns near Lafayette at the turn of the twentieth century. These have included the Bal du Mardi Gras (Mardi Gras Dance), which staged its first procession in Rayne on the second Saturday night before Mardi Gras in 1997; the inaugural Krewe de Mardi Gras Creole parade in Rayne on Fat

Tuesday 2000, which rolled for an estimated three hundred spectators; and Crowley's annual Carnival d'Acadie parade, which premiered on Fat Tuesday 2001 and had an estimated attendance of ten thousand just one year later.

11

Terrebonne and Lafourche Parishes

Deep in the heart of bayou country, near the Gulf of Mexico, the parishes of Terrebonne and Lafourche have extensive Carnival calendars that attract locals and visitors alike. Every year, the parades in Houma, Thibodaux, and surrounding communities consist of New Orleans–fabricated floats interspersed with marching bands and drill and dance units that help amp the spirit.

Paraders and spectators in Terrebonne and Lafourche parishes revel in their Creole, Acadian French, and Native American heritages of merrymaking and pride themselves on the exchange of exceptionally large quantities of souvenir throws. Maskers aboard the ten floats of King Sucrose's 1901 parade through Thibodaux tossed candies in profusion, and the parades of Ti Can Duplantis, rolling from Bayou Cane to Houma in the early 1900s, featured the throwing of sweetened popcorn balls. A 2016 preview of the Krewe of Hercules parade, largest in the two-parish area, indicates, obviously with some degree of hyperbole, the emphasis on numbers of floats and throws: "This year the krewe presents 35 double-decker floats carrying 750 revelers *bombing* crowds with *millions* of throws."[1]

Houma

The city of Houma, seat of Terrebonne Parish, features nine large parades and several elegant balls, and bills itself as host of the most extensive Carnival calendar outside Greater New Orleans. The town's earliest-known Mardi Gras parade rolled in 1911 and was led by banker Joseph A. Robichaux, who reigned as "King Bivalve" in honor of the local oyster industry.

Three years later, Filican "Ti Can" Duplantis, a Bayou Cane sugar-cane farmer, organized the Bayou Cane Carnival Association. Nearly every year from 1914 through 1930, Duplantis and friends transformed cane carts and hay wagons into floats and paraded through the Bayou Cane settlement on Bayou Terrebonne and often extended their route three miles down the bayou into the town of Houma.

The lengthy Bayou Cane parades are remembered for horse- and oxen-drawn floats decorated in cane reeds, palmetto, moss, and wildflowers, plus the appearance of a trained goat, monkeys, and other small animals in cages. Mountains of sweetened popcorn balls made by Madame Duplantis were tossed to spectators from a two-wheel cart drawn by Duplantis' own bull, Veidel. The 1924 parade featured twenty-five floats led by "King Boeuf," as Bayou Cane's live *boeuf gras* calf was known. In 1926, the *Houma Courier* estimated that 100 Bayou Cane "young people" belonged to the Carnival Association and that their parade attracted some 5,000–6,000 spectators from a two-parish area (Terrebonne and Lafourche) each year.

The spirit of the Bayou Cane Carnival parades spread down Bayou Terrebonne among the townspeople of Houma, and shortly after Ti Can Duplantis' 1924 festivities, the Houma Carnival Club was organized with the purpose of staging a "gorgeous" ten-float, New Orleans–quality parade. These preparations manifested themselves on Mardi Gras 1925 in the Rex parade led through the streets of Houma by King Bivalve. Houma's memorable 1926 celebration featured four parades. "Ti Can" Duplantis led his Bayou Cane Carnival Association three times from Bayou Cane into Houma—"a little more elaborate and gorgeous each succeeding day," according to the *Courier*—on the Saturday preceding Mardi Gras, again on Lundi Gras, and lastly on Shrove Tuesday itself. Fat Tuesday was also marked in the streets of Houma by the Junior Carnival parade of bands and floats carrying 150 costumed children, led by "Old King Cole" and following the theme "Mother Goose."

The extravagant 1926 Carnival celebrations in Bayou Cane and Houma appeared to be the last for a few years, a fact lamented by the

Courier in 1929. There was a Ti Can Duplantis parade in 1930, but it was the last one reported in Houma for several years. Then, from 1937 through 1940, Vic Maurin of the Fox Theatre organized the Kiddy Club, a procession of mini-floats and costumed children held on Fat Tuesday afternoon. In 1941, Houma Elementary School staged a similar event on the Monday afternoon prior to Mardi Gras. Lively, full-scale parades of floats were coordinated by the city's African American population on Mardi Gras afternoon in 1939 and 1940, and Mardi Gras Indians were noted at each of those celebrations.

Following the 1941 festivities, no parades were held in Houma until after World War II. The Houma-Terrebonne Carnival Club reintroduced a full-scale parade to the city on Shrove Tuesday 1947, and Carnival has been celebrated consistently in Houma since then. The 1947 parade, which rolled under overcast skies, included ten mule-drawn floats led by Hayes Henry as King Neptune, and had local Carnival pioneer Ti Can Duplantis as its grand marshal.

Houma's Carnival parades today feature New Orleans–built floats and generally include from three to eight marching bands as well as other units, some of which come from out of state. Houma's parades originally followed an east-west route from Grand Caillou Road to Main Street along Bayou Terrebonne, then across the Intracoastal Canal and into the downtown section. Since 1994, most of the krewes have followed a four-and-a-half-mile route running west to east from Southland Mall, following the bayou on Park and Main streets, and disbanding downtown. The Krewe of Mardi Gras, however, confines its route to a section east of the Intracoastal Canal.

Beginning in 1948 and continuing to the present, King Houmas, named for the local Indian nation, has ruled over the Fat Tuesday celebration. The Krewe of Houmas' first floats, brought in by barge from New Orleans, where they had rolled in earlier parades, were mule-drawn through 1950. Tractors, jeeps, and trucks have drawn the floats each year since. In 2016, when the parade rolled with eighteen floats, nine marching bands from near and far vied for prizes in the krewe's annual band contest.

Following in the wake of King Houmas on Mardi Gras afternoon is the Krewe of Kajuns parade, an annual feature begun by the local Jaycees in 1967. Originally parading with twenty or more large trucks, the Kajuns upgraded to conventional floats in 1997 and grew to feature as many as twenty-seven floats. With the emergence of other parade krewes in the city, however, the Kajuns' lineup was modified; in 2016, the krewe employed fourteen floats plus two additional floats independently entered. For many years, the Kajuns did not select and present royalty; at the turn of the twenty-first century, however, they began to choose an annual queen. Despite this and the krewe's conventional floats, many spectators continue to refer to the procession as "the truck parade."

The Krewe of Hercules, Houma's first and longest parade of the season, has since its inception in 1986 marched on the second Friday night preceding Mardi Gras. Founded as a men's krewe, Hercules opened its membership to women in 1991 and has stretched with as many as twenty-eight floats and eight or more marching bands. With its huge floats and abundance of throws hurled by enthusiastic riders, Hercules is nicknamed "Bacchus on the Bayou" after the great Bacchus parade in New Orleans. As might be expected, attendance on Hercules' night usually matches or exceeds that of Shrove Tuesday in Houma, estimated at 100,000 in years marked by optimal weather conditions.

Since 1995, the night of the second Saturday preceding Fat Tuesday has been marked by the parade of the Krewe of Aquarius. The initial number of twelve floats has increased to twenty, with four bands in this annual parade.

Houma's first female parade, led by the Krewe of Hyacinthians, debuted in 1952. Founded by the Ladies Carnival Club, the Hyacinthians originally paraded on the Thursday night preceding Mardi Gras. In 1959 they changed their rolling time to the afternoon of the second Sunday before Mardi Gras. Led by Queen Hyacinth, the popular parade stretches with nineteen floats and six or seven marching bands. The Hyacinthians parade is a perennial favorite owing to special floral touches on the royal floats and the enthusiasm of its riders. The year 2009 saw the inaugural

Krewe of Titans parade, which featured eighteen floats in the wake of Hyacinthians. A "family krewe" in that its riders are typically parents and their children, Titans grew to include twenty floats by the year 2015.

Aphrodite, a women's krewe that hit Houma's streets in 1984, parades on the Friday night before Mardi Gras. They were the first krewe to hold a night parade in Houma in more than twenty years. Aphrodite, officially the Houma Women's Carnival Club, rolls with twenty-two floats rented from the Krewe of Hercules. The two organizations therefore coordinate their annual parading themes.

The Krewe of Mardi Gras, open to male and female members, has held parades on the Saturday night preceding Mardi Gras since 1995 and has grown in length from seventeen to thirty-one floats. It is the only parade to roll on the less-populated east side of Houma, draws smaller and quieter crowds than on the city's "west" route, and is therefore especially popular with families.

The male Krewe of Terreanians has been a high point of Houma Carnival since 1951. The second-oldest men's krewe in the city, the Terreanians gained a reputation for throwing substantially more trinkets than its older kinsman, the Krewe of Houmas. Terreanians rolled on the Saturday night before Mardi Gras until 1961, when the parade switched to the Sunday afternoon preceding Fat Tuesday. Founded by the Greater Houma Carnival Club and now hosted by the Terre Carnival Club of Houma, the Terreanians featured eleven floats in 1965 and currently roll with twenty-one floats and usually three bands.

The nocturnal parade of the women's Krewe of Cleopatra has been a Houma attraction on Lundi Gras night since 1988. This parade now boasts twenty-two floats, which are occupied by both krewe members and other groups who pay for the privilege. This is not a feature unique to Cleopatra, either in Houma or outside the city, but Cleopatra is a good example of one parade containing riders of differing backgrounds. The slate of marching bands accompanying Cleopatra's floats grew through the years to include nine local and visiting school and jazz bands in 2016. A contest for best band performance is held each year.

Parades led by African American krewes have a sporadic history in Houma. From 1952 to 1958, Mardi Gras afternoon was marked by the parade of the Zulu Carnival Club, named after the famous New Orleans monarch. That krewe's place was taken in 1968 by the Taureans, who paraded for at least four more years before being discontinued. Even shorter lived was the Krewe of Tut, an African American group who paraded only twice—in 2009 and 2010—immediately following the Terreanians parade on the Sunday afternoon before Mardi Gras. In 2016, there were no specifically African American parades in Houma, but individuals from that culturally rich ethnic community have chosen to join krewes such as Mardi Gras in east Houma and Hercules in west Houma.

As early as 1949, attendance at the Krewe of Houmas parade was numbered by the local newspapers as high as 50,000 spectators. In 2000, Houma police officers estimated that each of the city's various Carnival parades would draw between 40,000 and 50,000 persons. One year later, in 2001, their expectation rose to between 60,000 and 70,000 for each parade. Beginning in 2005, krewe officials and law enforcement have numbered the Houma crowds at 100,000 for those parades rolling during favorable weather.

An online 2016 poll conducted by the sister sites www.houmatoday.com and www.dailycomet.com found that more than 53 percent of respondents attended no parades for the reason that they "don't like the crowds." According to the same poll, 30 percent frequented the Houma parades, 11 percent the parades in Thibodaux, 2 percent those of New Orleans, and 3 percent multiple cities, "the more the better." As the polled area consisted primarily of Terrebonne, Lafourche, and Assumption parishes, with a total population of more than 234,000 in 2016 per the US Census Bureau, it follows that more than 77,000 people attended Houma's parades, nearly 33,000 those in Thibodaux, and nearly 12,000 went to New Orleans.

Competition among Houma krewes and their members to hurl the largest and most trinkets of the season has, at times, resulted in accidents to bystanders. That, in addition to the custom of krewe members cruising the city streets in chauffeured "party buses" for hours before their actual parades begin, all the while imbibing alcoholic drinks and blaring music, have resulted in a shift of parade attendance by some residents from Houma to smaller celebrations, or their avoidance of the occasion altogether. In response, each year, Houma's krewe officials stress restraint among their membership, and Terrebonne Parish and assisting law enforcement agencies work to ensure that the "party bus" rides and parades are safe, that beads and other objects are not thrown too aggressively at spectators, and that incidents such as one float group's firing of a confetti cannon that knocked out part of the city's electrical system during a recent night parade are not repeated.

Carnival balls featuring tableaux and court presentations have been a Houma tradition since 1898. Today the parading krewes, as well as the non-parading Krewe of Flames, named in honor of the city's firemen, stage fine balls. Most of these still include tableaux and debutantes, though the tableaux largely tend to be humorous skits as opposed to the dramatic, often esoteric productions of the stately old krewes of New Orleans. Several Houma balls offer the opportunity for the public to attend, for an admission fee, if only to view the presentation of royalty and the tableaux. At other balls, participants and the public enjoy catered or self-prepared food and drinks of all kinds at tables set up around the presentation and dance floor.

Rural Terrebonne Parish

Though Houma is, by far, the hub of Carnival activities in Terrebonne Parish, its rural neighbors have long been in on the Carnival act as well. The second Saturday afternoon before Mardi Gras is marked in the community of Chauvin by the parade of the Krewe of Tee (for *petit*) Caillou, formed in 1985 and featuring from eleven to fourteen floats and two bands. During the early half of the twentieth century, Shrove Tuesday itself in this area consisted of costumed and masked residents promenading the length of the community with the aim of remaining unrecognized by their neighbors throughout the day.

Montegut has enjoyed a ten-float children's parade, usually accompanied by a local school marching band, on the Sunday afternoon preceding Mardi Gras since 1947. The 1955 festivities were canceled when Montegut's residents directed their efforts toward rebuilding the local Catholic church that had been lost to fire. The twelve-float adult Bonne Terre parade, which first rolled in 1972, began as a benefit for the children's parade and is held on Mardi Gras afternoon in Montegut. Indicating their adaptability, the Krewe of Bonne Terre rescheduled their parade in 2016 to immediately follow the children's parade on Sunday, as they unable to obtain a sufficient number of floats for Tuesday.

Erstwhile parades in Terrebonne Parish include those formerly held in Dulac and Bourg. Dulac established a parade on the Saturday afternoon preceding Mardi Gras in 1985 through the efforts of the pastor and members of the local Catholic church. The Krewe of Bayou Boulette assumed sponsorship of the event in 1993. Featuring as many as eighteen floats some years, the Dulac parade consisted of approximately eleven floats by the year 2002 and followed a four-mile route from Grand Caillou to Dulac. After Hurricane Lili struck the area in October 2002, the Krewe of Bayou Boulette discontinued its parade and ball. Bourg was the site of its own parade on the Saturday preceding Mardi Gras 2005: the Lil' Krewe of Gators.

Thibodaux

Carnival parades thrive with signature Cajun flavor in Thibodaux—seat of Lafourche Parish and the "Queen City of Bayou Lafourche"—and in the smaller towns along this waterway nicknamed "the Longest Main Street in the World." Local residents and visitors from nearby parishes who attend one or more of Thibodaux's parades each year cite the city's lengthy parade route as less crowded and relatively family-friendlier than those of nearby Houma and New Orleans.

The first known Mardi Gras parade on Bayou Lafourche was held in 1887 when "Rex's son, the King of Bulgaria," and his dukes representing various plantations of Lafourche Parish headed seven floats through the streets of Thibodaux. The area's first krewe, the Thibodaux Carnival Club, held parades led by King Sucrose from 1900 through 1906. The 1902 event drew a record fifteen thousand spectators. After the 1906 Mardi Gras, no parades were held until Fat Tuesday night 1914, when King Sucrose led seven floats in freezing weather for a crowd of six thousand spectators. Snow fell the following day. King Sucrose made his final appearance in 1915. Meanwhile, in 1914 and 1915, another king, the comical "Dodo," ruled over a separate Thibodaux parade.

There is little mention of any large-scale observance of Mardi Gras in Thibodaux from 1916 through 1954, though some form of parade was noted in 1922. Finally, in 1955, Mardi Gras returned to Thibodaux on a consistent basis with the inaugural Krewe of Chronos parade, whose ten floats and ten marching bands attracted an estimated ten thousand revelers despite rainy weather. Chronos grew through the years to include as many as nineteen colorful floats in its three-and-a-half-mile circuit of Thibodaux each Mardi Gras afternoon. Among Chronos' most coveted parade trinkets for many years were its signature plastic fried eggs.

By 1990, Chronos stretched with eighteen floats; in 2005, the number had scaled back to fifteen, and in subsequent years the number dropped to eleven floats. Similarly, Thibodaux's usual Mardi Gras attendance was pegged in 1982 at forty thousand, but by 1997 local police officers expected only twenty thousand spectators to line Chronos' route. Faced with further decreasing attendance—which civic authorities attributed to families leaving town for the extended holiday or attending larger cities' parades—Chronos made a dramatic, and appreciated, move in 2009 to the Sunday afternoon preceding Fat Tuesday. Of the various Carnival balls staged in Lafourche Parish, that of Chronos is most like the historic New Orleans pattern, with tableaux and court presentations, female court attendants and spectators wearing ball gowns and their male counterparts in the dignity of white tie and black tails.

The Krewe of Ambrosia has officially opened the Thibodaux parading season with as many as thirty floats and five bands since its inaugural procession in 1986. The parade rolled on the afternoon of the second Sunday before Fat Tuesday until 2012, when it switched to the night of the second Saturday before Mardi Gras. With this move, popular at first, night parading returned to Thibodaux for the first time since World War I. The repeated occurrence of cold weather and poor visibility for paraders and spectators alike and the resultant decline in membership and floats caused Ambrosia to return to Sunday afternoons in 2016.

Thibodaux's newest parade, led by the African American Krewe of Shaka, was first held on the Sunday morning before Mardi Gras in 1997. It switched to the second Sunday afternoon preceding Shrove Tuesday in 1999 and features as many as twenty-four floats and five bands from near and far. Each year, the king, queen, and court of Shaka as well as the krewe's officers appear in the parade in elaborate costumes of satin and velvet and feathered headdresses, a highlight of the Thibodaux Carnival calendar.

The Krewe of Cleophas, originally a men's krewe and nicknamed "the poor man's parade," held its inaugural parade with three floats in the wake of Chronos' 1957 parade and continued to parade through 1964. A new krewe named Cleophas debuted in 1971 as a family parade and rolled with six floats. In 1972, the krewe, stretching with fifteen floats, switched its rolling time to the Sunday afternoon preceding Mardi Gras.

Led each year by King Cleophas and Queen Clothilde (typical "old-time" French personal names), the lively parade grew to become "the biggest free show on Bayou Lafourche" and by 1997 stretched with forty-seven floats, likely a regional record. In 2016 Cleophas rolled with twenty-six floats and four bands. Popular both for the number of floats and the amount of throws cast by the riders, Cleophas draws the largest crowds of the Carnival season on Bayou Lafourche, pegged at nearly forty thousand in years marked by favorable weather.

Since Chronos moved to Sunday afternoon in 2009, Thibodaux's lone Fat Tuesday parade has been that of the Krewe of Ghana. Founded in 1973 by the Marvelettes Social Club, this festive African American parade featured ten floats and two bands its first year and grew to twenty krewe-owned floats redecorated according to new themes each year. Marching and strutting between the floats are second-line bands, dance troupes, and individual maskers in fantastic garb.

Ghana's floats are decorated in shimmering tinsel like those of Mid-City in New Orleans and the Lions parade in New Roads, and Ghana's royalty and krewe officers wear some of the most elaborate costumes outside New Orleans, with studded satin and velvet gowns and suits and feathered headdresses.

Ghana's krewe membership peaked at more than fifty in its heyday but dropped to seven by 2016. Most of its floats in recent years have been occupied by members of other local organizations and families. Despite the marked drop in Ghana's membership, its stalwarts have vowed to keep the glittering tradition going as long as they are able, and they successfully mounted a sixteen-float parade accompanied by two bands in 2016. Ghana spokespersons have claimed as many as fifty thousand spectators attended its parade, which could have been possible in its earliest years. The fewer parade-goers on Fat Tuesday in general, affected by Chronos' move to Sunday afternoon, mean a relatively uncrowded route and, therefore, lots of throws for Ghana's loyal followers.

Each of Thibodaux's parading krewes stages a ball with court presentations and tableaux. Additionally, the non-parading Krewe of Christopher has staged an annual ball in the city since 1953.

Elsewhere on Bayou Lafourche

Down Bayou Lafourche from Thibodaux, Carnival thrives in the towns of Lockport, Larose, Golden Meadow, and other bayou-front and inland communities. Many faithful attendees of the Houma and Thibodaux parades work into their Carnival calendars a visit to a parade or two in these smaller communities, where float riders tend to toss great amounts of throws to crowds smaller than those of the cities.

Presently, there are four parades in the Golden Meadow Carnival celebration. The excitement begins on the Friday night before Shrove Tuesday with the female Krewe of Athena parade, which premiered in 2012 with eleven floats. A fast grower, Athena rolls with seventeen floats and nine marching bands—the most bands seen in a Lafourche-Terrebonne-region parade in generations.

Since 1984, the Saturday afternoon before Shrove Tuesday has been marked by the parade of the "new" Krewe of Atlantis along a three-mile route in and near Golden Meadow. Though the annual event once featured as many as thirteen floats, its 2016 offering consisted of six floats and a ten-horse unit. Atlantis' ball is open to the public.

The female Krewe of Nereids began parading on the Sunday night before Mardi Gras in 1985. They long featured thirteen floats but increased the lineup to fifteen by 2004, also following a three-mile parade route.

Golden Meadow's oldest parade, that of the Krewe of Neptune, rolls at noon on Fat Tuesday. Since its debut in 1967, it has featured as many as fourteen floats but in 2016 rolled -with ten floats and two bands along its unusually long route. Stretching for five-and-a-half miles, it begins in the neighboring town of Galliano and goes through the entire length of Golden Meadow. In its earliest years of existence, Neptune received its floats by barge from New Orleans.

At midday on the Saturday before Mardi Gras, twenty floats bearing the co-ed Krewe of Apollo wind their way through the streets of Lockport, accompanied by one or two school bands from the area. The Apollo parade, a popular annual event since 1964, is sponsored by the Lockport Carnival Club. The parade is unique in that it is led, alternately, by a king one year and a queen the following year. No overall parade theme is set, so Apollo's float entrants may decorate their craft in any way desirable, which is the custom of community-oriented parades in even smaller burgs.

In Larose, on the afternoon of the second Sunday before Shrove Tuesday, the Krewe of Versailles, parading since 1975, takes a three-and-a-half-mile route from Larose into the neighboring town of Cut Off with as many as eighteen floats. The newest krewe to be founded in Larose, the Krewe du Bon Temps, held its inaugural parade on the Saturday night before Mardi Gras 2006. It features ten floats and is known to be especially generous with throws. Other Larose parades have included Babylon, which debuted with eight illuminated floats on the Saturday night before Mardi Gras 2002 and shifted its parading slot to behind that of Bon Temps with ten floats on a three-and-a-half-mile trek from Larose into Cut Off; and the Krewe de T-Kajuns, on the Sunday afternoon immediately preceding Mardi Gras, a children's organization that premiered in 2001 and grew to include approximately 250 riders aboard twenty-four floats.

On Fat Tuesday, the inland Lafourche Parish communities of Gheens and Chackbay are swarmed by bands of masked young men who chase children, order them to say their prayers, and playfully "whip" them with switches in a custom of pre-Lenten repentance said to date back to ancient times in Europe, if not earlier to the ritualistic flagellation of the ancient Roman Lupercalia. The Gheens and Chackbay parades are scheduled so as to give ample time for spectators to view one event, drive a relatively short distance, and view the other. The Gheens parade, an annual morning event since 1972, follows a three-mile route and usually consists of approximately twelve floats. Open to the public's participation, the Gheens parade only requires that entrants "have something to pull." Chackbay's observance dates back to the early 1900s and has been orchestrated since 1983 by the Krewe of Choupic as a parade of ten floats along a three-and-a-half-mile route. In the first decades of the twenty-first century, Choupic claimed to draw Lafourche Parish's largest Fat Tuesday attendance, estimated in excess of ten thousand.

Grand Isle, in neighboring Jefferson Parish, is host to the Independent parade, formerly known as the Jean Lafitte parade, on the Sunday afternoon before Mardi Gras. By the turn of the twentieth century, attendance at the annual parade, which includes units of various types, was estimated at five thousand by area officials.

Northwest of Thibodaux, Labadieville, in neighboring Assumption Parish, celebrates on Lundi Gras night with the ten-float parade of the Krewe of Xanadu. The first Xanadu parade rolled in icy conditions in 1989. Attendance has been estimated by parish officials at around seven thousand.

12

Elsewhere in Acadiana

St. Mary Parish

On scenic Bayou Teche, the lovely town of Franklin, seat of St. Mary Parish, was once an Anglo-Saxon enclave in the midst of French Louisiana. Nevertheless, for many years, the community has staged a mammoth Mardi Gras community parade, the origins of which date from the time of the visits of King Rex in 1926 and 1927. The 1926 parade, though "somewhat hastily arranged," stretched with more than forty floats depicting local industrial and business interests, with Wilson T. Peterman reigning as Rex and Winnie Roger as his Queen, according to the *St. Mary–Franklin Banner Tribune.*

In 1927, three parades rolled on Fat Tuesday: one at 10 a.m., perhaps the one described in a 1966 *Banner-Tribune* article as a walking procession staged by the local PanAm Bulk Station; the "Big Parade" of the Mysterious Babies Carnival Club, led by Rex, at 2 p.m.; and a nocturnal parade of the same floats at 8 p.m. Children's and adult balls followed the festivities.

After 1927, there appeared to be no further Mardi Gras parades in Franklin until the first arrival of King Sucrose, named for the local sugar industry, in 1934. King Sucrose I was represented by Kerall O'Neill and his Queen Sugar was Miss Margaret Bauer. Threatening weather failed to deter a crowd estimated by the media as high as twelve thousand for Sucrose's second visit, in 1935, when eleven floats and two marching bands participated. Between 1936 and 1946, no Mardi Gras parades were reported in Franklin, but news accounts continued to tell of Carnival balls, some years presided over by adults named King Sucrose and Queen Sugar and other years by high school students representing King and Queen Mars. King Sucrose permanently returned to the ballroom in 1947, and the next year he led Franklin's street parade, which continues to the present.

As a civic parade, the Franklin event differs from formal krewe parades, which usually build or rent a standard number of floats each year. The tally of floats in civic Carnival parades depends on the public's interest and participation and, therefore, has fluctuated from year to year. A float count in randomly selected Franklin parades, gleaned from the *Banner-Tribune,* reveals nineteen floats in 1948; up to a staggering fifty in 1954; down to seventeen in 1958; up to thirty in 1959, when the tossing of "throw aways" (or "throws") was mentioned; twenty-two in 1971; down to eleven in 1981, described as a "longer than usual" parade, suggesting a marked decline during the 1970s; and peaking at more than fifty floats in 2009.

Now billed as the "All Krewes Parade," Franklin's mammoth Fat Tuesday spectacle features participation by various Carnival organizations of the area, including the Krewes of Sucrose, the Teche, Agmarol (acronym for Agriculture, Marine, and Oil, Franklin's chief industries), Shona, and Guhmboh. The parade follows a mile-long route. *Acadiana Profile* magazine estimated Franklin's usual Mardi Gras attendance at fifty thousand by 1981, but two decades later, when perfect weather greeted the festivities in 2002, the local media pegged the crowd at fifteen thousand spectators. Exaggerations of early estimates aside, it is likely that the increase in the number of area parades in the late twentieth and early twenty-first centuries has caused a shift in revelers' destinations in the Bayou Teche area on the big day.

Record inclement weather in the form of freezing rain and resultant road and bridge closures spurred the cancellation of Franklin's venerable parade in 2014. Determined to observe the holiday in some fashion, the king, queen, and pages bundled up and took a short airboat ride on Bayou Teche to toss goodies to the few intrepid persons on the bank.

The third Saturday prior to Shrove Tuesday has been marked in Franklin since 1994 by the Head Start parade. Sponsored by the various

Head Start educational programs of St. Mary Parish, the parade includes marching bands and floats manned by Head Start students.

Several St. Mary Parish communities followed Franklin's lead in establishing Carnival parades in the mid-twentieth century. On the Saturday preceding Mardi Gras 1958, a parade of floats rolled from Berwick across the Atchafalaya River bridge into downtown Morgan City. In the twenty-first century, the popular Morgan City parade calendar, featuring New Orleans–type floats and marching bands, opens on the Friday night before Mardi Gras with the fourteen-float men's Krewe of Adonis parade, an annual event since 1976. Each of the floats has a specific throw. The female Krewe of Galatea, boasting one of the largest marching band lineups outside New Orleans, presents seventeen floats and as many as fifteen bands on the Sunday afternoon preceding Fat Tuesday. Galatea, which usually draws Morgan City's largest crowd of the season, has been an annual event since 1970.

The Morgan City Elks organization sponsored a twenty-five-float parade headed by King Cervus Ales I, whose queen was Miss Leta Prohaska, on the freezing Shrove Tuesday of 1914. However, parades on that day were not a consistent feature in Morgan City until 1960, when the Morgan City Fire Department Ladies' Auxiliary orchestrated the inaugural Krewe of Hephaestus parade. At present, fourteen floats interspersed with bands and other entries trace a two-mile route for Hephaestus' thousands of followers. Troy Landry, native of nearby Pierre Part and star of the popular television reality series *Swamp People,* reigned as King Hephaestus during the cold and wet Mardi Gras of 2014. The Siracusaville-Greenwood parade, an African American parade, has been an area attraction on Mardi Gras afternoon in the Morgan City suburbs of that name since 1995. It offers residents an alternative to the larger crowds in Morgan City proper.

Nearby, a unique krewe alternates its route from year to year between two towns, Berwick and Bayou Vista, on the Saturday preceding Mardi Gras. Founded as the Berwick–Bayou Vista Mardi Gras Association in 1977, the organization was renamed the Krewe of Dionysus in 2002.

Fifteen floats entered by a number of area krewes participate each year, and though the parade does not usually feature marching bands, sound systems interspersed throughout the parade provide the beat.

Amani, an African American krewe, first rolled on Lundi Gras afternoon in 1999 in Patterson. In 2002, it was rechristened as the combined Krewe of Amani-Hannibal. Leading the parade each year are King Amani and Queen Imara. Predictions of rain for 2005 led Amani-Hannibal organizers to postpone their parade to the first Saturday after Easter that year, a delay unseen in Louisiana since the 1990 Alla parade was postponed to St. Patrick's Day in Algiers.

In Charenton, the Chitimacha parade, named for the local Indian tribe, takes place on the Saturday preceding Fat Tuesday. Several floats and decorated vehicles normally comprise the lineup, which draws residents as well as visitors for a relatively low-key celebration.

Three parades debuted during the early twenty-first century in St. Mary Parish: the Baldwin Mardi Gras Association's parade in Baldwin in 2001 and the Cypremort Point parade in 2002, both on the Saturday preceding Fat Tuesday, and the Centerville parade, on Mardi Gras morning in historic Centerville. All are smaller-scale events than the parades of Franklin and Morgan City, particularly the Centerville parade, which is favored by families who want to celebrate Fat Tuesday in a calm and easily accessible environment. Baldwin's parade grew to nineteen floats, two bands, and sixteen other units in 2016, when the king's, queen's, and court friends' floats joined the lineup after the Newcomers parade in St. Martinville was canceled.

Iberia Parish

New Iberia, "Queen City of the Teche" and seat of Iberia Parish, enjoyed Mardi Gras parades led by Le Roi du Cypres (the King of Cypress) at the turn of the twentieth century. In 1948, the Krewe of Iberians held a single parade and never returned to the streets.

The Krewe of Andalusia, named in honor of the city's Spanish origins, has held a Carnival ball for many years and in 1993 reintroduced parading to New Iberia with a night parade on the Friday before Shrove Tuesday. Beginning in 2004, the parade rolled on the second Friday night before Mardi Gras. Twelve New Orleans–type floats and approximately a half-dozen bands constituted the Andalusia lineup, which usually attracted about ten thousand spectators along the mile-long route. By the second decade of the twenty-first century, costs of putting on the Andalusia parade had risen, according to krewe spokespersons, to as much as twenty-six thousand dollars, with the rental of floats alone being as high as fifteen thousand. These costs, plus rising rates for security and insurance, the retirement of longtime orchestrators, and lack of other members to assume their responsibilities resulted in the discontinuance of the Andalusia parade after 2015.

Just to the northwest of New Iberia is the community of Coteau, where the Krewe of Coteau held its maiden voyage on Fat Tuesday 2002. Unlike Andalusia, which was modeled after the parades of New Orleans, Coteau is a less expensive production, popular in that paraders and spectators are usually well known to one another.

Three Carnival parades are held in other areas of Iberia Parish. The African American Jeanerette Mardi Gras Association has rolled in that town on the second Sunday prior to Shrove Tuesday since 1994. Led by King Ezana and Queen Nefertiti, the parade features floats entered by about ten local organizations and two to four bands each year along a two-mile route. Attendees tout Jeanerette's parade among their favorites as crowds are relatively light—estimated at four hundred people for the fair-weather 2016 event—and larger throws such as stuffed animals are distributed along with the usual beads.

The old Creole farming enclave of Grand Marais, to the southwest of Jeanerette, began its public custom of celebrating Fat Tuesday in the 1940s, with outdoor cookouts and visiting among residents. In the 1970s, the citizens added parading to the day's schedule, with maskers in cars and trucks. Floats were introduced in 1979, and the event became a popular one with revelers from beyond the range of the community. The decoration of homes and lawns, a series of weekend parties, and costume contests for king and queen from among nine area krewes highlight each year's season, culminating on parade day. The participants' garb includes robes, suits, and headdresses. Headware includes glittered and feathered versions of crowns, sombreros, and ecclesiastical mitres.

In the early twenty-first century, the Grand Marais parade stretched with as many as nineteen floats, four bands, and other marching units along it mile-long trek. Attendance estimates by law enforcement agencies and parade organizers average around fifteen thousand to twenty thousand, depending on the weather. The Grand Marais Mardi Gras Association and its supporters have been unluckier in weather than other Louisiana Carnival revelers. The 2013 parade was canceled due to rain forecasts. In the following year, freezing rain prevented the festivities from taking place. In the third consecutive year, cold and wet conditions prevailed again, with members parading rather spontaneously aboard trucks.

Loreauville, east of New Iberia, began staging a community-oriented parade at the close of the twentieth century. Known successively as the Papa Red Dog parade and the Family Affair Mardi Gras parade, it provides local residents a relatively calm Fat Tuesday observance, with much recognition between roadside onlookers and participants.

St. Martin Parish

Charming St. Martinville, seat of St. Martin Parish and the historic heart of Acadiana, held several Mardi Gras parades between 1894 and World War I. Early sponsors included the Board of Trade, which staged the parades of 1894–1900, 1902, and 1907, each headed by King Commerce; and the Woodmen of the World, who held parades in 1915 and 1916. The 1897 event drew a record crowd, estimated at six thousand, and the 1915 parade, with twenty floats, was the town's largest until the twenty-first century.

Following a long lapse, Mardi Gras merriment returned to the streets of St. Martinville in 1963 with the inaugural Newcomers parade, staged by the town's African American residents. Featuring a long line of floats of various types, marching bands, and other units, the Newcomers parade, on the Sunday prior to Shrove Tuesday, attracts the largest of the Carnival crowds along Bayou Teche. Floats are entered by area organizations and families, and local marching bands and dance troupes march between them. Former residents appreciate the parade as a convenient and festive time to return home for a visit.

By the early twenty-first century, local police estimated a crowd of ten thousand at the Newcomers parade but pegged the 2006 gathering at thirty thousand, attributing the increase to the number of families who moved to the area in the wake of Hurricane Katrina. With as many as twenty thousand standing four to five rows deep for subsequent parades, city and law enforcement officials became increasingly aware of the need for curbside barricades and additional security. In the midst of such considerations, no parade was held in 2016 owing to a court ruling that the city's parade permit was, in its stated form, unconstitutional.

In the eastern part of St. Martin Parish, in the great Atchafalaya River Basin, two communities stage Carnival festivities. The Lake Fausse Pointe State Park parade, including bands and dance troupes as well as rolling entries, travels through the park, on Levee Road near St. Martinville. As this is a state park, there are admission requirements. The Henderson community, a year-round rendezvous for fishermen, inaugurated the Henderson Heritage parade on the Sunday preceding Mardi Gras 2003. It followed an aquatic route, with paraders boarding boats and passing by the fishing camps of their supporters. The event was discontinued for a few years but was revived in the form of a street parade in 2016.

Vermilion Parish

Today, Vermilion Parish continues to be recognized by cultural anthropologists as well as local residents as one of the most "French" regions of Louisiana. Many people speak French, and their ethnic pride is readily evident in the town of Kaplan, the site of one of the state's most colorful Mardi Gras afternoon events since 1954. Led each year by royalty dubbed King Gumbo and Queen Jambalaya after two of the state's most identifiable—and delicious—foods, the parade is sponsored by the Krewe of Chic-a-la-Pie, named for the old French chant *Mardi Gras, chic à la paille,* meaning "Mardi Gras, as stylish as a scarecrow!"

Kaplan's parade is unique in Louisiana with float titles in French and riders donning old-fashioned masks and traditional capuchons, which originated as a spoof of European headwear. Chic-a-la-Pie is an especially long parade, with approximately sixty floats. Within thirty years of its inaugural run, local law enforcement officials estimated attendance of thirty thousand to fifty thousand, but as in other South Louisiana communities, figures were lower by 2002. In years marked by optimal weather conditions, crowds have ranged from twelve thousand, according to the local visitors' bureau, to twenty thousand, as reported by the print media.

Smaller-scale, community-oriented parades in Vermilion Parish have included the Krewe de Bon Temps parade, which premiered on the Sunday preceding Fat Tuesday 2000 in Pecan Island, and the Krewe of Vermilion children's parade, which first rolled in Erath on the third Sunday preceding Mardi Gras 2002. In the parish seat of Abbeville, Mardi Gras had not been celebrated for about forty years due to a city ordinance outlawing masking after a masked robbery occurred in the city one Fat Tuesday. The council lifted its ban in 2004, however, and the Krewe of Vermilion moved its venue to Abbeville to roll on the second Sunday preceding Mardi Gras.

One of the newest Carnival events in the area is held in Gueydan on the second Saturday preceding Mardi Gras. This joint production of Le Krewe du le Originales et Les Enfants and the Gueydan Duck Festival Association includes a chicken chase, parade of riders through town, food, music, and dancing.

* * *

St. Landry Parish

Long known for rural Mardi Gras celebrations, St. Landry Parish now enjoys street parades as well. In 2000, the Half-Fast Krewe of Frank's, named for its sponsoring business, became the first parade on Fat Tuesday in Opelousas since 1903. Frank's parade grew to include thirty units by 2016, and its attendance has been pegged as high as five thousand. Frank's parade is a good example of a community-oriented, open-to-all, participatory event. Its entries range from rented, themed floats, like those seen in nearby Lafayette and other larger celebrations, to flatbeds with minimal decorations. Emphasis is placed on the tossing and catching of throws and just having a good time for those area residents who elect not to attend the day's larger, more elaborate, and/or more distant celebrations. Opelousas' Carnival activities were supplemented in 2015 by an equestrian parade and chicken run, designed along the lines of the more rural Carnival celebrations. Held on the Sunday prior to Mardi Gras, it grew by its second year to include floats, marching bands, dance troupes, and all-terrain vehicles.

The Washington Mardi Gras parade is another open-to-all event, and since 1999 has been held in the charming town of that name north of Opelousas on the Sunday preceding Shrove Tuesday. Two other St. Landry Parish communities hold small but equally appreciated parades on the weekends before Mardi Gras: Melville since 2005, and LeBeau since 2007. The Melville event premiered as a fundraiser for the town's fire department, with six floats and two bands in the inaugural lineup. In LeBeau, an old Creole community, events center on the local Immaculate Conception Catholic Church.

Calcasieu and Jefferson Davis Parishes

The seat of Calcasieu Parish, Lake Charles is home to more than sixty krewes, a number surpassed only by New Orleans. The city's oldest krewes include Cosmos, founded in 1951; Contraband, 1963; Omega, 1966; Mystique, 1973; Des Amis, 1979; Barataria, 1979; La Famille, 1979;

and Grande Bois, 1980. Each krewe stages an annual ball, with its own king, queen, and court. These longtime krewes also participate in the Krewe of Krewes parade on Mardi Gras night, as do Lake Charles krewes formed in later years. Lake Charles is the only known city in Louisiana where the public may see the elaborate costumes of all local krewe courts in one place: on Twelfth Night (January 6) and again at the Royal Gala on Lundi Gras evening at the Lake Charles Civic Center. The city's tourism bureau calls the Royal Gala the "Cinderella night of Mardi Gras."

Lake Charles' earliest parade, that of Momus, King of Mardi Gras, was staged in 1882 for an estimated 1,500–2,000 onlookers. Following this single event, the annual observance of Fat Tuesday in the city was limited to school and fraternal organization balls and pageants for nearly a century. During the 1930s, the rural Courir de Mardi Gras festivities were introduced to the area by French families moving in from the Acadiana parishes to the east.

Street parades resumed in Lake Charles with the Krewe of Omega, organized in 1966, rolling on the Saturday afternoon before Mardi Gras; the Merchants parade on the following afternoon; and the Krewe of Krewes parade, inaugurated by Mardi Gras of Imperial Calcasieu in 1980, on Shrove Tuesday night. Subsequent changes in the Lake Charles Carnival calendar resulted in the children's parade being staged on the Sunday afternoon before Fat Tuesday, the Merchants' "Parade de Louisiane" on Mardi Gras morning, and the Krewe of Krewes and Krewe of Lake Charles parades on Mardi Gras night. By 2005, the Lake Charles Carnival calendar had been adjusted again to feature the Merchants parade on Friday night, a children's mini-parade and a lighted boat parade on Sunday, and the Krewe of Krewes parade on Mardi Gras night.

The Krewe of Krewes parade, rolling along a four-mile route, drew crowds estimated by organizers as high as 80,000–100,000 in 1991, and a liberal 300,000 in the twenty-first century. If accurate, current figures would be higher than those of Lafayette, which has consistently been touted as the state's second-largest Fat Tuesday celebration in attendance. Riders estimate that the forty-two-float lineup stretches for three-quarters of a mile and that each float carries five thousand gross of beads. Lake Charles' parade floats range from New Orleans–type creations to eighteen-wheeler truck floats and smaller floats pulled by automobiles. In Jennings, the seat of Jefferson Davis Parish and located east of Lake Charles, the Krewe of Bon Manger ("Good Eating") premiered in 1983. This parade rolls on the afternoon of the second Sunday before Fat Tuesday. Smaller, community-oriented parades were established in two towns near Lake Charles in 2002: one on the second Saturday before Mardi Gras in Lake Arthur, Jefferson Davis Parish; and another on the Saturday afternoon before Mardi Gras by the Krewe de Vatis in Vinton, Calcasieu Parish. They feature a sense of personal familiarity between paraders and spectators.

SOURCES FOR PART II: *The Advertiser,* Lafayette; Frances and John Love, *Allons a' L'Acadie* (Lafayette: Tribune Printing Plant, 1957); *Houma Courier; Houma Guide; Gumbo Guide,* Houma; *Thibodaux Commercial Journal; Daily Comet,* Thibodaux; *Bayou Life Magazine,* Donaldsonville, vol. 1, no. 1 (1996); *Banner-Tribune,* Franklin; *St. Mary Banner,* Franklin; *St. Mary-Franklin Banner Tribune; Weekly Iberian* and *Daily Iberian,* New Iberia; *Weekly Messenger,* St. Martinville; *Teche News,* St. Martinville; *Daily World,* Opelousas; *American Press,* Lake Charles; *The Advocate,* Baton Rouge; *Acadiana Profile,* Lafayette, vol. 4, no. 4, and vol. 8, no. 1, 1982; Florence Blackburn and Fay. G. Brown, eds., *Franklin Through the Years* (Franklin, 1972); Nora Mae Wittler Ross, *Mardi Gras in Calcasieu Parish: A Pictorial History* (Sulphur, La.: Wise Printing Co., 1991); Harnett T. Kane, *The Bayous of Louisiana* (New York: William Morrow & Co., 1941); Carl Lindhal and Carolyn Ware, *Cajun Mardi Gras Masks* (Jackson: University Press of Mississippi, 1997); Harry Oster and Reven Reed, "Country Mardi Gras in Louisiana, *Louisiana Folklore Miscellany,* January 1960; Louisiana State Office of Tourism, Calendar of Events; www.gomardigras.com; livinglifecajunstyle .com/mardi-gras-2014-in-gueydan-la; visitlakecharles.org/events-festivals/mardigras; loui siana.kitchenandculture.com/louisiana-mardi-gras-parade-schedule.

Rex, King of Carnival, upon his float still used today,
passes through crowds on Canal Street in the 1940s.

(Courtesy State Library of Louisiana)

Framed in blazing flambeaux, Comus toasts his queen and the courts
of Comus and Rex (*upper right*) at the Boston Club
on Canal Street on Mardi Gras night 1934.

(Courtesy State Library of Louisiana)

The Boeuf Gras float in the Rex parade symbolizes the actual animal
butchered, cooked, and eaten at the end of Carnival
and in advance of Lenten fasting.

(Courtesy Margaret Lovecraft)

This Rex parade float embodies the design and costumes of yesteryear.
(Courtesy Margaret Lovecraft)

The crowned figure at the front of this Rex parade float
is characteristic of early float artistry.

(Courtesy Margaret Lovecraft)

The Krewe of Proteus, founded in 1882, holds the state's second oldest
Carnival parade and continues to fashion its floats according to
high nineteenth- and early twentieth-century standards.

(Photo by author)

In the private realms of the New Orleans Carnival ball krewes, elaborate and longstanding rituals include tableaux, grand marches, and the presentation of bouquets to honored debutantes.

(Courtesy Mary J. Langlois)

Foldout invitation to the Rex Ball of 2011.

(Author's collection)

A 1930s Zulu king and attendants aboard their royal float.
(Courtesy State Library of Louisiana)

Marching Zulu members in familiar tribal regalia are always a crowd pleaser.
(Courtesy Margaret Lovecraft)

Riders on superkrewe "superfloats" are on level
with spectators on second-floor balconies.
(Courtesy Louisiana Office of Tourism)

The New Orleans Society of Dance's Baby Doll Ladies parade in the lively tradition of early twentieth-century predecessors.
(Courtesy Margaret Lovecraft)

Jazz musicians lead marching groups along their parade routes or offer
impromptu concerts on French Quarter streets.
(Courtesy Louisiana Office of Tourism)

Disguised riders and children with a prize chicken mark
Courir de Mardi Gras at Church Point in the 1970s.
(Courtesy State Library of Louisiana)

Colorful costumes and traditional capuchons typify
rural Acadiana Mardi Gras.

(Courtesy Country Lane Photography)

Courir celebrations in some communities include improvised floats
in addition to equestrian riders and maskers chasing after prize chickens.

(Courtesy Country Lane Photography)

Homemade wire masks, a staple of early nineteenth-century disguises, may still be seen in several southwest Louisiana Mardi Gras celebrations.

(Courtesy Country Lane Photography)

In many Louisiana communities, such as Mamou pictured here, Carnival celebrations draw the largest crowds of the year.

(Courtesy Country Lane Photography)

King Gabriel toasts Queen Evangeline during a
Lafayette Mardi Gras of the late 1930s.

(Courtesy State Library of Louisiana)

Female maskers in antebellum attire prepare to ride
in Hyacinthians parade in Houma.

(Courtesy Matthew Noel/Houma Area Convention and Visitors Bureau)

St. Joseph Co-Cathedral on the parade route in Thibodaux is a reminder that Carnival is the precursor to the penitential season of Lent.

(Photo by author)

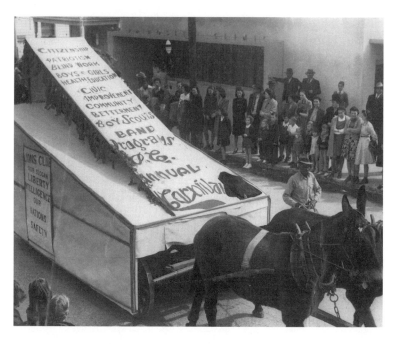

In 1942, New Roads' two parades were the only ones to roll for Mardi Gras, all others in the state having been canceled due to World War II.

(Author's collection)

Whimsical floats bearing youthful riders typify New Roads parades.

(Courtesy *Pointe Coupee Banner*)

A children's greased-pig chase follows
Courir de Lundi Gras on Raccourci-Old River.

(Courtesy *Pointe Coupee Banner*)

Iberville Parish Library royalty includes the Gray Monkey;
his wife, Brownie; and their baby, KoKo.

(Courtesy Iberville Parish Library)

The Krewe of Yazoo precision lawnmower brigade is a highlight
of Spanish Town and Southdowns parades in Baton Rouge.
(Courtesy Laura Gleason)

The Prancing Babycakes perform in Baton Rouge's Spanish Town parade.
(Courtesy Brandon M. Dufrene)

At the 2010 Krewe of Southdowns ball in Baton Rouge,
Queen Kate Kane Laborde and King Angus "Gus" Wilkes (*left*)
are presented with hand-made aprons by former queen Sherry Wilkes
(2006) and former king Kevin Stuart (2009), reflecting the
theme "Southdowns Is Really Cooking."

(Courtesy Laura Gleason)

The Krewe of Dionysus, founded in 1985, provides one of Slidell's most popular parades, shown here during the 2012 festivities.

(Courtesy Will Avera)

Madisonville and Slidell are among the communities that hold boat parades during Carnival. Shown here is the Krewe of Bilge Parade.

(Courtesy Slidell Mardi Gras Museum)

Dancers sporting purple, gold, and green boas greet spectators
at Alexandria's Children's Parade.

(Courtesy Alexandria-Pineville Convention and Visitors Bureau)

King Janus tosses beads into the night
during Monroe's Carnival parade.

(Courtesy Krewe of Janus)

Old-time South Louisiana capuchon, costume, and stilts combine
to make a memorable highlight of the Harambee parade in Shreveport.

(Courtesy Jim Noetzel/Shreveport Convention and Tourist Bureau)

Shreveport's counterpart to South Louisiana's Boeuf Gras is a
huge bull in an Old West setting, as seen on a Krewe of Centaur float.
(Courtesy Jim Noetzel/Shreveport Convention and Tourist Bureau)

A trailer bearing costumed band members amps up
Shreveport's Highland Parade.
(Courtesy Amy Lynn Treme/Shreveport Convention and Tourist Bureau)

Many Louisiana cities host pet parades during Carnival,
including Shreveport's Barkus and Meoux.

(Courtesy Jim Noetzel/Shreveport Convention and Tourist Bureau)

PART III

SOUTHEAST LOUISIANA

G eographic neighbors yet distinctive in their history and culture are the parishes that comprise southeast Louisiana, spanning from Pointe Coupee Parish in the north to St. Charles Parish in the south, and from West Baton Rouge Parish in the west to St. Tammany Parish in the east. The River Parishes, located along the Mississippi River between New Roads and New Orleans, have attracted generations of visitors enthralled both by the antebellum plantation homes, ranging from venerable Creole raised cottages to pseudoclassical mansions, and by a population of long residency whose tenacity in retaining old customs, including Carnival celebrations, is proverbial. In the twentieth century, this same area became known as the chemical corridor because of its riverfront industry. Louisiana's capital, Baton Rouge, is both a river city and the seat of a Florida parish. The eight Florida Parishes, extending from the Mississippi River to the Mississippi state line, form what was once the Republic of West Florida. Annexed by the United States in 1810, the region became part of the new state of Louisiana in 1812. The Florida Parishes boast a mixed cultural heritage but have especially deep Anglo-American roots.

13

New Roads

Among all the cities and towns staging New Orleans–style Mardi Gras festivities, the Creole French town of New Roads on scenic False River stands out distinctly in its organization and its history. Seat of Pointe Coupee Parish, New Roads was founded contemporarily with New Orleans, with a recorded settlement in the area since 1720. Unlike in New Orleans, however, New Roads' parades developed as civic events open to public participation. Though the city's two parades and related activities are indeed social statements, they are not staged by krewes and are of, by, and for the community at large and its visitors. They were among the first—if not the very first—to be racially integrated, since at least 1953, when the famed marching band of historically black Southern University took part in the predominantly white Lions parade.

Local organizations, schools, churches, families, and businesses build the New Roads floats personally for entry in the parade, and the children of the float builders are typically the maskers who ride the floats. Much of the construction cost is covered by donations from the business sector and dedicated citizens. Only in the selection of parade royalty and in the naming of the various committees needed to stage the event do New Roads' two parading groups function exactly like the New Orleans krewes.

As early as 1956, when the *Register* magazine featured a lengthy article titled "A Bow to the Town of New Roads," Louisianians as well as visitors have been captured by the traditions and festivity of the Mardi Gras celebration held in this town:

> And New Roads knows how to have a party or a celebration! Never is a festivity a token affair with only a few citizens participat-

ing. In this town when an occasion is celebrated, the whole populace takes part. Political rivalries, business rivalries, personal feuds, which are inevitable where a group of people exist, are temporarily abandoned and everyone cooperates for the success, the gaiety and pleasure of the occasion. . . . The Mardi Gras parades in New Roads have become something of a tradition in high quality and though the floats are built by amateurs they have a professional look—each a masterpiece in design, color, detail, and originality. . . . It is perhaps the thoughts of times past which give that extra sparkle and something out of the ordinary to New Roads celebrations. For tradition is preserved, yet innovations are not denied.[1]

As in the rest of French Louisiana, references to the early observance of Mardi Gras in New Roads and Pointe Coupee Parish, in the late nineteenth and early twentieth centuries, are of masked individuals and groups, some on horseback and others on foot, parading without any particular organization. But in this area, riders are not begging for communal gumbo ingredients as is the case with the Acadian French parishes to the southwest. The tradition of equestrian riders wending through the rural byways of Pointe Coupee was continued by the extended Decuir family and friends, who rode through the rural communities of Lakeland, Rougon, and Glynn and into adjacent West Baton Rouge Parish. The demise of older members of the group and increased demand for law enforcement in New Roads' rapidly growing Mardi Gras venue resulted in discontinuing this annual Shrove Tuesday tradition in the early 1980s.

In the town of New Roads, Mardi Gras balls are recorded as early as 1881, and the first known parade—two mule-drawn vehicles sponsored by Mayor Harry Demouy—rolled in 1897. On the first float, Demouy presided as Rex, surrounded by retainers brandishing instruments of the pharmacy trade, in advertisement of his New Roads drugstore. The second float carried a brass band. In 1910 and 1911, African American citizens presented parades of mule-drawn floats and brass bands, the 1911 procession being led by King Snowball and his consort.

Mardi Gras has been an annual event in New Roads since 1922, when local merrymaker Jimmy Boudreaux began the tradition of the town's Fat Tuesday morning parade with a single mule-drawn float and a brass band. Boudreaux's celebration grew to include two separate parades during the late 1930s and early 1940s: one on Lundi Gras night and the main parade on Mardi Gras morning. The morning parade in those years began with the arrival of the king and queen by royal yacht on False River, having come from the mythical "Island Paradise of Negrito." After the temporary suspension of all Mardi Gras parades during World War II, Boudreaux and friends resumed only the morning parade in 1946.

After Jimmy Boudreaux's death in 1949, there were no morning parades in New Roads for two years, but the tradition was revived by dedicated citizens in 1952. Officially the Community Center of Pointe Coupee Carnival parade, it is one of the oldest and largest African American–sponsored events in the nation and it is the state's oldest Mardi Gras parade after Rex, Proteus, and Zulu.

Records of New Roads' morning-parade royalty are complete beginning with 1949, when Patrick Nelson and Miss Ann Gaines ruled. In addition to floats and marching bands, the Community Center Carnival parade has always counted a large number of dance units and maskers on foot, the latter singly or in groups and dressed in garb ranging from the elaborate to the grotesque.

New Roads' second parade, held on Mardi Gras afternoon, began as the Children's Carnival parade, sponsored by the town's oldest women's organization, the Mothers Culture Club, from 1932 through 1940. The first king and queen were first cousins Marshall Gosserand Jr. and Marie Anita Hunter. In 1941, J. T. Niland and other local businessmen assumed sponsorship of this parade to raise funds for the purchase of band uniforms for a local school. King O. B. Laurent Jr. and Queen Jeanette Major, high school seniors, headed eight floats and four bands that inaugural year, with a crowd estimated at ten thousand. Three months later, Niland and friends formally organized as the New Roads Lions Club, and the organization has sponsored the afternoon parade ever since as a charitable fundraiser. High school seniors ruled over the Lions Carnival through 1948, after which adult rulers were chosen. From that point, the kings have been active New Roads Lions members and the queens college-age daughters of Lions. The first adult rulers, in 1949, were A. B. Curet and Miss Frances Lieux.

In 1942, New Roads' two Carnival parades were the only ones rolling, those in New Orleans and elsewhere having been canceled due to the war. Neither of New Roads' parades rolled during 1943–45, however, owing to material shortages and in deference to the war effort. Sleet in 1978, subfreezing weather in 1986 and 1989, freezing rain in 2014, and rain in many other years kept would-be revelers at home, but New Roads' parades rolled on undaunted. The severity of the weather in 2014 caused road and bridge closures and numerous automobile accidents throughout the region, resulting in a much smaller than usual parade attendance of about 20,000 intrepid supporters.

New Roads has a normal population of about 6,000, but the annual attendance at its Mardi Gras ranks as among the largest after New Orleans. Weather permitting, 100,000 or more revelers are estimated by parade and law enforcement officials to congregate in the town. The majority come from the Baton Rouge area and nearby southwestern Mississippi. The parade route has been modified and lengthened through the years to accommodate the growth, and the present three-mile route and the abundance of off-street parking add to the convenience.

Floats entered in the competitive category adhere to themes chosen annually by the Community Carnival and Lions clubs. What they may lack in size, New Roads' floats make up in creativity. Built fresh each year, they are decorated with a profusion of colored foil and petal paper and often sport features such as smoke-breathing papier-mâché dragons and bubbling volcanoes, confetti-firing cannons and calliope music.

New Roads parade throws of the 1960s–80s consisted of candy, bubble gum, small plastic toys, and miniature loaves of bread baked and wrapped by the Holsum Bread Company of Baton Rouge. In recent decades, New Roads' throws have greatly improved in quantity and quality—long-strand metallic beads and imitation pearls, logo doubloons, go-cups, stuffed animals, posters, and Bayou State novelties such as plastic crawfish, alligators, and "shrimp boots."

The 1970s and 1980s were marked by diminishing parade participation, with an average of twelve floats and three bands per parade, due to a tightened local economy and the consolidation of area schools, each of which formerly had its own band. Since then, however, New Roads parades have grown greatly in length, owing to a renewed interest in the celebration and an abundance of security for paraders and parade-goers alike. Civic and law enforcement officials, parade organizers, and the general public recognize Mardi Gras as Pointe Coupee Parish's major tourist draw and have increased their support of the annual event.

By 2016, each parade included as many as thirty-five floats and nine marching bands, plus military and ROTC units, dance teams, school and club royalty, and comic mini-vehicles. At the rear of each parade are the truck floats, called "comic floats" in New Roads, which feature rollicking "Mardy Graw" merrymakers and music. Lions Carnival parade-goers of the 1950s recall comic float riders as including men masked and dressed as women, with generous "padding" front and rear, who would periodically dismount from the floats and dance with unsuspecting male spectators.

Parade royalty and its secrecy are among the most hallowed traditions of New Roads Carnival, touted for generations as "Pointe Coupee's Best Kept Secret." Anonymous committees of the Carnival and Lions clubs select their ruler and court about five months prior to each Mardi Gras. The identity of the courts is made known shortly before parade day, but the kings and queens remain anonymous until Mardi Gras itself, when they are ceremoniously unmasked before their club's reviewing stands during the parades. The Community Center Carnival organization and the New Roads Lions hold costume balls on the weekends before Mardi Gras—the Community Center on the Saturday preceding Shrove Tuesday and the Lions on the second Saturday before Mardi Gras. Admission is open to the public at both.

Near New Roads

In the northern part of Pointe Coupee Parish, the Krewe of New California paraded on Mardi Gras afternoon from 1979 through 2004, with the exception of 2003. Participants rode horses, bicycles, and other vehicles as well as modest miniature floats in a more subdued atmosphere than the New Roads celebration. A king and queen were chosen annually, and attendance at the event was numbered as high as one thousand before the parade was discontinued due to declining participation.

Carnival festivities resumed in the Batchelor area with the inaugural Courir de Lundi Gras, a procession of mounted maskers and decorated all-terrain vehicles and mini-floats. The first courir was held in 2011, and each year since, hundreds of spectators have gathered to witness the parade disband and to engage in public dancing and feasting on the banks of Raccourci–Old River.

The southern Pointe Coupee Parish town of Livonia began its annual Carnival parade in 1984. Sponsored each year by the Livonia Carnival Association and open to public participation, the parade is held the Sunday afternoon preceding Mardi Gras. As many as twenty-two floats roll along with the town's high school band, and attendance at the parade peaked in its early years at about ten thousand. Recent attendance has been about four thousand, the decline due to the growth in the number of parades in other communities on the same weekend, according to law enforcement officials.

Following the New Roads pattern, a king and queen are secretly selected to reign over the Livonia parade and post-parade private reception; their identities remain secret until their unmasking during the parade. The 2012 Carnival made history as it was ruled by two queens—twin sisters Blakely and Brooke Chauvin—a first-known event in all of Louisiana Carnival history. As with the New Roads Lions, the annual Livonia court is composed of local high school students.

South of Livonia and just across the border in neighboring Iberville Parish, the town of Maringouin is the site of two predominantly African American parades, both of which are open to public participation. They roll on the Saturday afternoon preceding Mardi Gras. The first parade, the Krewe of Maringouin, premiered in freezing weather in 1989. The 2015 parade had fourteen floats. In the wake of the Krewe of Maringouin comes the Krewe of Athena, which debuted in 2014. When the Krewe of Maringouin was the sole parade, normal attendance was estimated at three thousand. According to police officials, the addition of Athena to the afternoon's festivities has upped the turnout considerably.

14

Baton Rouge

Long before Carnival parades became a regular feature of Baton Rouge's festive calendar, pre-Lenten balls highlighted the capital city's social scene. Since the mid-twentieth century, readers of Baton Rouge's print media have been able to view the resplendent royalty in all their glory and read accounts of the balls held on previous nights. Moreover, Baton Rougeans have a better chance of attending balls and other indoor events and of being accepted to krewe membership than their counterparts in New Orleans. The oldest ball krewes in Baton Rouge include Tucumcari, Romany, Iduna, Achilles, Desk & Derrick, Lyonesse, Camelot, Apollo, Bon Temps, and Karnival Krewe de Louisiane. Many began as rather small affairs and grew to include hundreds of members, extensive courts, tableaux, and members' guest lists.

Baton Rouge's oldest krewe, Tucumcari, was founded by residents who, while vacationing in Tucumcari, New Mexico, learned the romantic legend of Native Americans Tocum and Kari. Tucumcari's first ball was held in Louisiana's capital city in 1948. Formed as a couples' krewe, it became all male as some of the wives began to form their own krewes in 1949. Romany is the oldest of the female krewes, from which some members separated and formed Iduna in 1960.

The Mystic Krewe of Achilles is Baton Rouge's second-oldest male krewe, having premiered in 1956. The Krewe Mystique de la Capitale was Baton Rouge's first co-ed krewe, staging its first ball and a parade in 1976. The Krewe of Apollo premiered in 1981 as a fundraising organization to assist victims of HIV/AIDS. In 1987, Karnival Krewe de Louisiane, a co-ed organization, held its inaugural ball as a fundraiser for Mary Bird Perkins Cancer Center. Other krewes founded during the late twentieth century that stage balls include Spanish Town, Artemis, Orion, and the now-defunct Jupiter and Juno.[1]

Unlike the old-line Carnival balls of New Orleans, Gabriel in Lafayette, and Chronos in Thibodaux, which are all white-tie-and-tails events, most Baton Rouge balls are black-tie events, though they surpass the old New Orleans krewes in elaborateness of court costumes as well as tableaux, usually adhering to each year's theme. Another difference is that the capital-city krewes often adopt Hollywood-like, musical, or other easily recognizable and flashy themes. Like New Orleanians, though, many Baton Rougeans place much emphasis on their own Carnival royalty and its traditions and consider their balls the highlight of the social season.

Louisiana senators, representatives, staff members, and families in Washington, DC, have staged and participated in the Mystick Krewe of Louisianians ball, which has been staged, with a few lapses, each Carnival season since 1944. The ball is self-funded from admission fees, corporate sponsorships, and krewe members' dues. The "Washington Mardi Gras Ball," as it is commonly known, attracts as many as three thousand revelers for dancing, viewing of tableaux, and presentation of royalty. Congressman F. Edward Hebert and Miss Mollie Gaumer, a member of Senator John Overton's staff, reigned as inaugural king and queen in 1944. Beginning in 1948, many of Louisiana's annual harvest-festival associations have sent their queens to participate in the ball, adding to its glamour.[2]

Baton Rouge was a relative latecomer in taking Carnival to the streets. Nocturnal parades were held by the city's Young Men's Business Club during 1949–56, rolling on Mardi Gras night 1949–55 and on Lundi Gras night in 1956. Seven to nine floats were featured each year, along with as many as fourteen bands and presiding royalty, but the parade was discontinued after repeatedly being dogged by rain and cold weather.

Generations of Baton Rouge families have been loyal attendees of Carnival parades in other cities, particularly in New Orleans, New Roads, and Lafayette on Mardi Gras day. After a two-decade absence of Carnival parades in the capital city, the Krewe Mystique de la Capitale initiated a parade in 1976 that continues each year on the second Saturday before Mardi Gras. Mystique originally rolled on Florida Boulevard, Baton Rouge's principal retail thoroughfare at the time. With downtown renovation projects and the establishment of new parades downtown at the close of the twentieth century, Mystique changed its route to follow suit. A dozen krewe floats built in the New Orleans fashion and adhering to each year's theme, plus another ten or so floats entered by other groups, constituted the usual Mystique lineup for many years. In 2016, Mystique rented and rode eighteen floats owned by Plaquemine's Krewe of Comogo. Mystique spokespersons have lamented the inability to procure a sufficient number of, if any, marching bands on what is an increasingly active parade day throughout Louisiana.

The Saturday before Mardi Gras brings the zany Spanish Town parade, an annual event since 1981. The parade had humble beginnings as a walking procession on Highland Road, with a king brandishing a meatball impaled on a long fork as a scepter. It became a much larger production and attracted more spectators once it moved to the Spanish Town neighborhood near the Louisiana State Capitol. Winding for two miles and for several hours through the downtown area, this satirical parade boasts of being an untraditional Carnival affair with an annual theme, individual float subjects, and often risqué costumes and throws. Past themes have included "Louisiana's Dirty Laundry," "LA Purchase—Name Your Price," "FEMAture Evacuation" (a spoof on the Federal Emergency Management Association's response to the Hurricane Katrina crisis), and "XXXpress It." Spanish Town kings have run the gamut from convicted former Louisiana governor Edwin Edwards to a dog named "Rubin" to retired local children's television-show host, "Buckskin Bill" Black.

As many as seventy large truck floats, interspersed by such entries as lawn-mower and folding-chair "brigades" of marchers, draw a spirited public who celebrate with food and alcohol long before and after the parade. The Spanish Town crowd, estimated by the media at 30,000 in its earliest years, grew to a record 100,000 according to board member Bruce

Childers when ideal weather marked the 2013 event. With such an attendance, the Spanish Town parade is, after Louisiana State University foot-
ball games and associated tailgate partying, Baton Rouge's largest event.
The plastic pink flamingo, billed as the ultimate in tackiness, is the
official symbol of the Spanish Town parade, and its appearance at various
places in the city, including the waters of City Park Lake, heralds each
year's parade and the annual Spanish Town ball. A well-attended event at
the Baton Rouge River Center, open to the public for an admission fee,
the ball is famed for its excesses in costumes and celebrating. Attendees
can rent tables and stock them with food and drink for the show.

Considerably more sedate than Spanish Town is the family-friendly,
illuminated parade in the Southdowns subdivision near Perkins Road.
First held in 1988 on the night of the Spanish Town parade, the Southdowns parade switched its date to the Friday night before Mardi Gras in
2002. The lineup includes as many as twenty-two floats and five marching bands, and the relatively uncongested route is popular with families
who wish to take in the experience of a nighttime Carnival parade.

At the dawn of the twenty-first century, the number of Carnival parades in Baton Rouge quickly increased. Most are composed of New
Orleans–style, individually themed floats carrying costumed and masked
krewe members. Popular among Carnival revelers is the female Krewe
of Artemis, which was founded in 2003 and soon grew to sixteen floats.
Artemis rolls through downtown Baton Rouge on the second Friday
night preceding Fat Tuesday. The male Krewe of Orion defied a downpour to premiere with a fourteen-float, seven-band New Orleans–style
parade on the second Saturday night preceding Fat Tuesday in 2000.
The lineup quickly increased to seventeen floats and thirteen bands, and
Orion is a perennial favorite among capital-city parade-goers, both for
the creativity of the floats and the generosity of float riders in dispensing
throws. It bills itself and is largely appreciated as the most New Orleans–
like parade in the city and can be viewed with little of the congestion
of the Crescent City parades. Not to be outdone by Lafayette's Krewe
des Chiens and other canine Carnival parades, the dogs of Baton Rouge

may costume and revel, along with their owners, in the Mystic Krewe of Mutts parade, held along tree-lined North Boulevard downtown on the second Sunday before Mardi Gras. Participation is open to the public.

Artemis, Mystique, and Orion follow an identical three-mile route along several streets of downtown Baton Rouge. Spanish Town rolls along a shorter route, but Spanish Town Road is usually packed from building line to building line, often ten rows deep. As such, Spanish Town is obviously the largest-attended Carnival event in the capital city. Assessments of the various parades via video and photographs in years marked by comfortable weather reveal crowds five rows deep near the formation points of the Artemis, Mystique, and Orion parades on River Road, with less congestion in other areas, and suggest approximately 45,000 persons. Spanish Town's crowds are considerably larger, as evidenced by the same sources and in parade organizers' and law enforcement estimations, normally approximating 100,000 spectators.

The Krewe of Jupiter, a male krewe, presented its New Orleans–style parade of floats and bands and a ball in 2004. In 2011, it became a co-ed organization, the Krewe of Jupiter and Juno, and paraded through 2014. A membership decline from 200 to 45 resulted in the discontinuance of both parade and ball.

Shorter-lived, neighborhood parades in Baton Rouge include the Chaneyville parade, which first rolled on the Saturday before Fat Tuesday 2004; the parade of the Krewe of Gus Young, a civic organization named for a late African American community leader, which first rolled on the second Saturday afternoon preceding Mardi Gras 2005; and the Westminster–Pine Park parade, which held its first run on the second Sunday before Mardi Gras 2006. North of Baton Rouge, the city of Baker held its inaugural parade in 1996, on the afternoon of the third Saturday before Mardi Gras.

15

St. Tammany and Other Florida Parishes

Historic Clinton, seat of East Feliciana Parish, began the tradition of its Feliciana Family and Friends parade, held on the second Saturday before Mardi Gras, in 2006. Floats are entered by area organizations and families, while other participants have included equestrian units and the outstanding Southern University marching band from Baton Rouge.

East of Baton Rouge, three parades are held in Livingston Parish. Springfield, on the Tickfaw River, holds a boat parade, the Krewe of Castaways, on the second Saturday afternoon before Fat Tuesday. Since 1981, the town of Denham Springs has also held a parade on the second Saturday afternoon preceding Fat Tuesday. As many as fifteen floats have been featured throughout its history. Head of Island, located on the Amite River and Diversion Canal, is the site of a boat parade sponsored by the Krewe of Diversion on the second Sunday afternoon preceding Shrove Tuesday. Proceeds of the boat parade benefit the St. Jude Children's Research Hospital. All of these are community-oriented events, in which area organizations and families participate, and there is much friendly recognition between paraders and spectators.

Tangipahoa Parish also hosts three parades. In the town of Ponchatoula, the Krewe of Pericles launched its maiden voyage on the second Friday night preceding Mardi Gras 2005. The Krewe of Omega rolls through the city of Hammond on the second Friday night prior to Shrove Tuesday. The krewe's hundred-plus members aboard a dozen floats are joined by other entries and participants in this parade that first rolled in 1987. The Krewe of Aliases, Hammond's second parade, debuted behind Omega in 2002. These parades offer something of the

151

Carnival City flavor, but with easier ingress and egress to the communities and family-friendlier settings.

On the Northshore of Lake Pontchartrain, St. Tammany Parish has an extensive and lengthy Carnival calendar with many of its parades in the New Orleans tradition, featuring themed floats, royalty, marching bands, and large quantities of throws. The size of St. Tammany's towns and parade crowds relative to New Orleans', however, are perennial evidence that many Louisiana Carnival-goers prefer smaller celebrations in family-friendlier settings.

Parades begin on the fourth Sunday before Mardi Gras with the Krewe of Claude, founded in 1986 and rolling in the city of Slidell with thirteen floats. Immediately following is the Krewe of Poseidon, a male and female group founded in 2015, aboard twenty-three floats. The St. Tammany Parish parade schedule then unfolds as follows.

Third Saturday before Mardi Gras: The Krewe of Bilge boat parade starts at noon, an annual tradition in Slidell since 1977. At night, the Krewe of Mona Lisa and Moon Pie, founded in 1985, marches on foot through Slidell.

Third Sunday before Mardi Gras: In Slidell, the Krewe of Slidellians, founded in 1961 and featuring female members aboard eight floats; and Perseus, a male and female krewe established in 1971 riding thirteen floats. In the community of Pearl River, the Krewe of Pearl River, founded in 1953 and sponsored by the local Lions Club as a charitable fundraiser.

Second Friday night before Mardi Gras: Eve, a twenty-four-float female krewe parading through the streets of the scenic lakeshore town of Mandeville. This annual tradition premiered in 1987.

Second Saturday before Mardi Gras: In the morning are two events: the comic Krewe of Push Mow, in which marchers push decorated lawn mowers through the town of Abita Springs, and the Krewe de Paws, a pet parade in Slidell open to the public. At night, Olympia, a male krewe aboard eighteen floats, processes through the lovely town of Covington. Simultaneously, the Titans, a male and female krewe, ride twelve floats through Slidell.

Second Sunday before Mardi Gras: Dionysus, founded in 1985 and one of the area's largest parades, features twenty-four floats bearing a male krewe through the streets of Slidell.

Friday night before Mardi Gras: Selene, a female krewe that premiered in 1999, parades aboard eighteen floats in Slidell. At the same time, the "Original" Orpheus parade rolls in Mandeville on twenty-four floats. Founded in 1988, the procession predates the Orpheus parade of New Orleans; hence the Mandeville organization added "Original" to the name of its Northshore krewe.

Saturday before Mardi Gras: Tchefuncte, a boat parade on the Tchefuncte River at the town of Madisonville, is one of the parish's noted popular Carnival traditions, taking place since 1973. The parade is preceded by a promenade of King Neptune's Marching Society to the official reviewing stand.

Shrove Tuesday: Two parades roll in the town of Covington. The Lions parade, established in 1959, stretches with as many as seventy-five rolling and marching units. Immediately in its wake follows the Mystick Krewe of Covington, formerly known as Kaa Cee (for its sponsors, the local Knights of Columbus), founded in 1952 and rolling with ten floats.

In the late twentieth and early twenty-first centuries, a number of other Fat Tuesday parades premiered in St. Tammany Parish, many having brief or sporadic histories. Among those continuing are the very informal Bush parade in the community of that name; the Krewe of Skunks, in Lacombe, with approximately fifteen floats; and Chata, founded in 1990 and rolling with approximately twenty-five floats, also in Lacombe. "Chata" is the nickname of the beloved nineteenth-century Catholic missionary to the local Native Americans, Abbé Rouquette. The erstwhile parade of the Krewe of Folsom was held in the St. Tammany Parish community of that name on Shrove Tuesday from about 1971, with some lapses, until finally disbanding in 2003. A community-based production in the fullest sense, this event featured decorated pickup trucks and equestrian entries and provided area families with a Fat Tuesday alternative to larger celebrations.

Near the eastern state line, the town of Bogalusa, in Washington Parish, is the site of the lengthy Magic City Carnival Association (MCCA) parade on the Saturday before Shrove Tuesday. The MCCA parade debuted in 1980 with six floats and grew rapidly. In the early twenty-first century, the parade stretched with as many as thirty-three floats, fifteen marching bands, and eight drill units, earning it the nickname of "the biggest small town parade." Further north, the Washington Parish seat of Franklinton entered the Carnival parading scene in 2004 with two parades: the Krewe of Franklinton on the third Thursday night before Mardi Gras, and the Krewe of Pepe on the Sunday before Fat Tuesday. These are community-oriented events.

16

The River Parishes

Just across the Mississippi River from Baton Rouge, the town of Port Allen, seat of West Baton Rouge Parish, has enjoyed a parade on the Sunday afternoon before Mardi Gras since 1985, compliments of the Krewe of Good Friends of the Oaks. Floats are built and entered by various local groups and families. An estimated ten thousand spectators attend the parade annually, according to law enforcement officials.

The parish's oldest Carnival event, the Firemen's Carnival parade, has provided pre-Lenten fun to the residents of Addis and surrounding areas on the second Sunday afternoon before Mardi Gras since 1963. By the late 1990s, attendance was estimated by local police officers to have peaked at five thousand, and in 2004 the lineup included nineteen floats. In the custom of civic-oriented parades, the floats are built and entered by area businesses, organizations, and families. The early twenty-first century was marked by fewer floats and smaller crowds in Addis due to the proliferation of other communities' celebrations, according to spokespersons, but the Addis event remains a popular alternative for families.

Plaquemine, seat of Iberville Parish, is home to three lavish Carnival balls: Du Roi ("Of the King"), Okeanos, and Cypress, all of which are known far beyond the boundaries of the city for their elaborate costumes and spectacular tableaux. Kings sporting wings, borne in litters, and entering the ballroom on horseback have provided enduring memories for ball-goers. Though attendance at the balls is by invitation only, the general public may view the introductory court presentations and tableaux of all three events from grandstands above the ballroom floor.

As a South Louisiana community of considerable early wealth, owing to its sugar and cypress-lumber industries, Plaquemine has, sporadically, been the site of street parades through the generations. The town's earliest Carnival parades included the Komical Klan of Komus, which rolled in 1880 and 1881. King Cypress (unrelated to the Krewe of Cypress of the late twentieth century) headed parades in 1904–5, 1907, 1915–17, and 1921. Subsequently, the local fire department staged torch-lit automobile parades on Lundi Gras night in the late 1920s and 1930s, with floats and bands added to the lineup in the 1950s. The parade was discontinued shortly thereafter, as the town's citizens have consistently preferred the ball tradition over that of parading.

On the Friday prior to Shrove Tuesday, local schoolchildren march in the Gray Monkey mini-parade, named for its costumed, stuffed-animal "king." Established in 1946 by Plaquemine Elementary School first-grade teacher Lolita Daigre, the parade was discontinued for some time but was revived by the local library in 1985. The Plaquemine Community parade, largely an automobile event, has been staged on the Saturday afternoon before Shrove Tuesday by African American residents since the early 1990s.

Plaquemine residents long hoped for the return of full-scale parades of floats and bands to the city, with local ball designer Ms. Brenda Comeaux and friends attempting to launch a night parade of at least eight floats at the close of the twentieth century. Finally, on Lundi Gras night 2013, the first Krewe of Comogo paraded in Plaquemine with thirteen New Orleans–style lighted floats, undaunted by rainfall. The krewe is named in memory of Comeaux, who had meanwhile succumbed to a long illness. A fast grower, Comogo rolled along its two-and-a-half-mile route with sixteen krewe-owned floats for an estimated ten thousand spectators who braved near-freezing weather in its second year. Comogo increased to eighteen floats and five marching bands in 2016 as attendance rose to an estimated thirty thousand to forty thousand from throughout the region, according to law enforcement officials. Comogo, envisioned as an annual Lundi Gras procession, has adapted its rolling night as needed: in 2015, to the preceding Sunday night to avoid predicted rain;

and to the second Sunday night before Mardi Gras 2016 in deference to televised coverage of the Super Bowl on the preceding day.

Historic Donaldsonville, seat of Ascension Parish, has sporadically celebrated Fat Tuesday with parades since 1900. "Roi, the Rice King," led eleven floats through an estimated ten thousand spectators in 1902, after which there were no parades until King Mohawk, also at the head of eleven floats, paraded for some five thousand in 1917. In 1923, King Progress ruled supreme, and his parade attracted a record twenty-five thousand people. For several years, beginning in 1928, King Zulu led a parade through Donaldsonville. In the 1950s, festivities were centered on a children's parade sponsored by St. Vincent Academy, with a record forty-two mini-floats rolling in 1956.

The Industro parade was staged in Donaldsonville from 1968 through 1980, premiering with sixteen floats for more than eight thousand spectators. Shrove Tuesday was subsequently observed in Donaldsonville by the parades of the Krewe of Sisters in 2003 and the Mystic Krewe of Mardi Gras in 2004 and 2005. The following decade saw no parades in the city, but the annual Krewe of Elks ball, an elaborate invitational event, maintains the Carnival spirit for Donaldsonville residents and those of surrounding communities. Presided over by King Jolly Fellow and his Queen, the ball features a court and presentation of area debutantes. Though held in Donaldsonville for most of its history, the ball venue was moved to the Assumption Community Center in nearby Napoleonville by the time of the eighty-second annual fete, in 2015.

In the eastern part of Ascension Parish, across the Mississippi River, the Krewe of St. Amant stages a parade of decorated boats on Diversion Canal in the community of St. Amant on the second Sunday afternoon prior to Mardi Gras. Riders cast beads and other favors to spectators lining the banks, in the same manner as street parades.

Lutcher, in St. James Parish, held its first Carnival parade, the Krewe of Save De Children, on Mardi Gras afternoon 2002. This parade was formed by community members committed to providing a safe, family-oriented celebration as a form of character guidance. More recently, the Krewe of Tomorrow paraded in the contiguous towns of Lutcher and Gramercy on Mardi Gras afternoon 2016.

St. John the Baptist Parish hosts two parades. In Reserve, the truck parade of the Krewe of Towahpasah premiered on the Saturday afternoon before Fat Tuesday in 1997 and grew to become a procession of fifteen standard floats and automobiles in 2016. In LaPlace, the Krewe Du Monde ("Krewe of the People") has been a popular tradition since 1973 for thousands of area residents and visitors on the Sunday afternoon preceding Shrove Tuesday. Du Monde grew to include as many as twenty-four floats in the 1990s before being reorganized and rolling with fourteen floats and six marching bands in 2004. By 2016, under the sponsorship of the LaPlace Lions Club, the number of floats rose to twenty-seven, bearing seven hundred riders. That year, a new feature in the form of a drum line was added to the lineup. Du Monde attracts a large attendance, not only from the immediate LaPlace area but from surrounding parishes as well, as many parade-goers prefer its less-crowded setting to that of New Orleans parades on "Mardi Gras Sunday." During the season, Du Monde stages a ball, open to the public, with proceeds benefiting the local Lions' charities.

In St. Charles Parish, King Lul leads the parade in Luling on the Saturday afternoon before Shrove Tuesday. Floats are built fresh each year by various neighborhood krewes, and the procession follows a rectangular route through town. Held since 1976, Lul stretched in 2016 with twenty-five floats, the local high school marching band, and a half-dozen dance troupes. A grand marshal, king, and queen are selected to lead each year's parade.

The town of Des Allemands' celebration, held on the Sunday afternoon before Mardi Gras, began in 1959 as a function of the local American Legion post and was originally called by acronym the AmLe parade. Now coordinated by the local Lions Club, the parade is known as the Krewe of Des Allemands parade. It is open to public participation and features twenty or more floats on its annual 2.7-mile trek. Floats adhere to no specific parade theme, and no royalty are chosen. Like the Lul parade on the preceding day, Des Allemands provides considerably less crowded and family-friendlier merriment for Mardi Gras weekend.

SOURCES FOR PART III: *Pointe Coupee Banner*, New Roads; *State-Times*, Baton Rouge; *Morning Advocate*, Baton Rouge; *The Advocate*, Baton Rouge; *The Chief*, Donaldsonville; *Iberville South*, Plaquemine; *Plaquemine Post South*; *Gumbo Guide*, Houma; *Daily Comet*, Thibodaux; *Daily Courier*, Houma; Arthur Hardy Enterprises, *Mardi Gras Guide;* louisiana.kitchenandculture.com/louisiana-mardi-gras-parade-schedule.

PART IV

CENTRAL AND NORTH LOUISIANA

While the Carnival celebrations of Central and North Louisiana do not have histories as long as—and therefore, as much recorded information as—their South Louisiana counterparts, the popularity of parades in Alexandria, Monroe, Shreveport, and surrounding towns indicates that Carnival is indeed a "tradition in the making" in the upper portion of the state.

17

The Alexandria Region

In the hub city of Central Louisiana—Alexandria—the public celebration of Carnival came into being in 1994 with the birth of the Alexandria-Pineville Mardi Gras Association. Twenty years later, the association had grown in membership to more than two thousand local residents. Each year's Carnival season begins on January 6 with a gumbo dinner and merrymaking. A large-scale Winter Ball is held later in the month. These events are followed by balls hosted by the twenty-five krewes that have been formed in the area since 1994.

The Mardi Gras Association selects three local humanitarians to serve as grand marshals of its three parades each season. On Friday evening before Mardi Gras, the Hixson Classic Cars & College Cheerleaders parade rolls, followed by the Taste of Mardi Gras culinary event, featuring signature local delicacies such as meat pies and barbecue. As its name implies, the parade consists principally of cheerleader squads from Central and North Louisiana colleges along with classic automobiles, but the lineup also includes floats, military personnel, and, of course, beads and candy as throws.

Saturday has been marked since 1997 by a children's parade downtown. A king cake party follows at one of the region's popular visitor attractions, the Alexandria Zoo. The largest and oldest parade of the association trio, the Krewes parade, features twenty-two floats manned by the various area Carnival organizations on the Sunday before Mardi Gras. Organizers say that the parade's rolling date was set specifically to avoid conflicts with the large, long-established events on Shrove Tuesday. Alexandria's Carnival events draw considerable crowds, with the association estimating peak attendance in 2015 at 120,000 for the Krewes parade and 25,000 for the children's parade.

There are also smaller-scale parades in the Alexandria area: on the second Saturday before Mardi Gras, the Krewe of Woodworth parade in the community of that name, an annual event since 2000, and the Krewe of Pollock children's parade, held in Pollock since 2006; on the Wednesday before Mardi Gras, the LSUA parade, which rolls at midday through the Alexandria campus of Louisiana State University; and on Shrove Tuesday afternoon, the Krewe of Provine parade, which premiered in Alexandria in 2005. All four are family-friendly events with easy access to the parade routes and much familiarity between paraders and spectators.

The newest area parade is the Light the Night parade, which premiered in 2015. Held on the second Friday night before Mardi Gras, the parade forms and travels through Pineville, across the Red River, and into downtown Alexandria for disbanding. Revelers are met by a brass band near parade's end as the finale of the celebration.

Avoyelles Parish

Though geographically considered part of Central Louisiana, Avoyelles Parish forms the northern apex of Louisiana's ethnic and cultural French Triangle, and its residents demonstrate a particular fondness for perpetuation of the French language and customs. Its settlement began with Creole French and Native American residents of Pointe Coupee fleeing the Mississippi River floods of the 1780s and continued through emigration of French families from Mother France well into the late nineteenth century. Like their contemporaries in South Louisiana, Avoyelles citizens of all ages during the late nineteenth and early twentieth centuries observed Mardi Gras by costuming and perambulating the rural neighborhoods. From time to time, Carnival balls, complete with kings, queens, and courts, were staged in the parish seat of Marksville.

Street parades, a relatively new feature of Carnival in the Marksville area, provide an opportunity for families to partake of the pre-Lenten merriment with relatively easy access and smaller crowds. The Krewe of Kids premiered in the village of Fifth Ward on the Sunday afternoon prior to Mardi Gras 1997. On the rainy second Sunday before Mardi Gras 1998, the Krewe of Cyllenius debuted in Marksville. The following year, this same organization rolled as the Krewe of Cronus in Bunkie and has continued to alternate name and location in this fashion.

Other Avoyelles Parish communities staging Carnival parades in recent years have included Moncla and Simmesport. The parades in Avoyelles are civic rather than formal krewe events. Open to public participation, they include floats of varying elaborateness, decorated vehicles, equestrian groups, and the customary candy, beads, and other trinkets for the spectators.

Natchitoches

The beautiful and history-laden town of Natchitoches, located on the Cane River and seat of Natchitoches Parish, is a Creole French enclave in the middle of predominantly Anglo-Saxon, Protestant upper Louisiana. The town is promoted as the oldest in Louisiana, established as a military post by Pierre Juchereau de St. Denis in 1718. Oral tradition tells of masked balls held by older members of the community in the nineteenth century, but it was not until the late twentieth century that the city was home to a full-fledged krewe. In 1978, thirty-two members of the Mystic Krewe de St. Denis staged their first tableau ball. By the first decade of the twenty-first century, the organization had doubled in number and its annual events included a Twelfth Night Party and Queen and King Party in addition to the ball. Natchitoches' first known Carnival parade, that of the Krewe of Dionysus, premiered in 1995 on the Saturday night preceding Fat Tuesday. It now draws thousands of spectators annually to view twelve or more large floats bearing the three-hundred-member krewe.

Some thirty miles to the northeast of Natchitoches is Winnfield, the seat of Winn Parish and the birthplace of late governor Huey "The Kingfish" Long. Winnfield hosts the Krewe of Kingfish parade on the Saturday evening before Mardi Gras. Since the parade's inaugural run in 1993, local organizations and families have built and entered floats in competition for prizes and tossed trinkets to their supporters along the route.

18

Monroe and Surrounding Areas

Well outside the realm of French Louisiana, cities and towns in the northern part of the state inaugurated public Carnival celebrations in the twentieth century. In Monroe, Mardi Gras was first observed in the 1930s by costumed African Americans masquerading in their partially segregated neighborhoods. Little is known of any subsequent Carnival celebration in the area until 1985, when the Twin Cities Jaycees presented the first Krewe of Janus parade. Its name suggestive of the cities of Monroe and West Monroe, located opposite each other on the Ouachita River, the parade rolls on the second Saturday before Mardi Gras from West Monroe, over the Ouachita River bridge, and into Monroe proper.

Janus became an organization independent from the Jaycees in 1989 and grew considerably, with the number of New Orleans–type floats in the annual procession reaching thirty-five. Six high school marching bands are slated for each year's parade, which is financed through the Monroe–West Monroe Convention and Visitors Bureau, and prizes are awarded to the top performing units. By far the largest annual event in the region, Janus has seen attendance increase from 35,000 in its inaugural year of 1985 to 175,000 by 2013, according to krewe representatives. Janus hosts its black-tie Grand Ball on a weekend early in the Carnival season. Tickets are available to the public for purchase.

In the twenty-first century, two other events joined Janus on the second Saturday before Mardi Gras: the Krewe of Janus's children's parade of marchers and cyclists in the morning, held indoors in Pecanland Mall shopping center; and the Krewe of Paws canine parade in the afternoon along the city's downtown Antique Alley, a tradition since 2008. Both events are open to public participation.

Located near the Mississippi River and equidistant from Monroe and Alexandria (approximately eighty miles) is historic St. Joseph, seat of Tensas Parish. St. Joseph held its first civic Carnival parade on the Saturday night before Mardi Gras in 2004.

19

Around Shreveport

The Shreveport–Bossier City metropolitan area, located on Louisiana's upper Red River, has fully embraced the Carnival season. Today it boasts fifteen krewes and several full-scale parades that together attract an estimated 400,000 parade-goers, according to event organizers.

The Krewe of Centaur parade, which rolls on the second Saturday
night prior to Mardi Gras, premiered in Shreveport in 1992. Stretching
with thirty large floats bearing five hundred members who throw some
1.5 million trinkets, Centaur is by far North Louisiana's largest Carnival
parade. Krewe spokespersons state that the organization's name was chosen to represent the mythological half horse–half man in recognition of
the horse-racing and gaming industries of the Shreveport–Bossier City
area. Though officially "Centaur," krewe members refer to their organization familiarly as the "Fun Krewe."

One of the earliest events of the Carnival season in Shreveport is the
Krewe of Harambee Mardi Gras/MLK Day parade, held on the Martin
Luther King holiday and therefore honoring both the champion of civil
rights and Louisiana's Carnival traditions. An especially lengthy parade,
it is noted for its large number of area high school and university marching bands, stilt walkers, and dozens of rolling entries in its annual trek
through the downtown area.

The Krewe of Sobek, also a predominantly African American organization, was founded by nine individuals in 2003 and named for an Egyptian deity. The krewe held its first ball in 2004 and first street parade in
2005. The organization bills itself as the "Premier Mardi Gras Krewe of
Northwest Louisiana" and celebrates on the fourth weekend preceding
Mardi Gras with a Friday night "Grande Bal" featuring tableaux and

court presentation and a Saturday parade through the Queensborough neighborhood of Shreveport. Ball attendance and parade participation are open to the public.

The Krewe of Highland, founded in 1995, also features a parade and ball open to public participation. The parade rolls on the Sunday afternoon before Mardi Gras in the Highland neighborhood of Shreveport, with some of its floats rented from the Krewe of Centaur.

The Krewe of Gemini sponsors Shreveport–Bossier City's oldest Carnival parade and ball, which have formed a highlight of the pre-Lenten season in the Ark-La-Tex (contiguous corners of Arkansas, Louisiana, and Texas) region since the krewe's premiere in Bossier City in 1990. The parade, held on the Saturday before Mardi Gras, debuted with twelve floats and has grown to include more, plus bands and, in krewe parlance, "millions of throws" for its onlookers.

The local pet parade is cleverly named the Krewe of Barkus and Meoux, a play on the names of New Orleans' Bacchus superkrewe and Muses female parade. Held at Reeves Marine Center on the second Sunday preceding Mardi Gras, this family-oriented celebration is open to the public with the costuming of participating pets encouraged.

For twenty-four years until 2014, the area's final parade of the Carnival season was that of the Krewe of Asclepius, named for the god of healing and composed of medical professionals of the Ark-La-Tex region. This organization, which focused on entertaining children of the community, paraded around Pierre Bossier Mall shopping center, with the option of moving into the mall itself in times of inclement weather.

About forty-five miles north and east of Shreveport is Springhill, seat of Webster Parish. Springhill holds its Main Street Mardi Gras parade on the third Saturday prior to Shrove Tuesday, an annual event since 2005. Oil City, thirty miles northwest of Shreveport, held its first Carnival parade on the third Saturday before Mardi Gras 2006, compliments of the Krewe of Caddo Parish. Thousands of spectators were estimated to have viewed the 2016 parade.

SOURCES FOR PART IV: *Avoyelles Journal*, Marksville; *Daily Town Talk*, Alexandria; *News-Star*, Monroe; *Shreveport Times*; *Natchitoches Times*; *Winn Parish Enterprise*, Winnfield; *The Derrick*, Oil City; *The Advocate*, Baton Rouge; Louisiana State Office of Tourism, Calendar of Events; alexmardigras.com; www.pineville.net/egov/docs/1452827266187.html; www.monroe-westmonroe.org; www.louisianatravel.com/articles/mardi-gras-shreveport-bossier-city; www.mystic-krewe-de-saint-denis.com; louisiana.kitchenandculture.com/louisiana-mardi-gras-parade-schedule; www.myneworleans.com/Louisiana-Life/January-February-2016/Around-Louisiana.

Epilogue

The many facets of Carnival in twenty-first-century Louisiana reveal tradition and spontaneity, ostentation and economy, restrained dignity and raucous abandon. Its long history has seen Carnival develop from unorganized masking, to elaborate parades and balls of the elite, to events more accessible to the general public. It has withstood tests of political change, socioeconomic strain, natural disasters, and changing tastes. An adequate assessment was made in *New Orleans Magazine*'s online "Krewes News" during the 2016 season: "Carnival is like a big balloon: colorful, ever expanding, but always seeming somewhat vulnerable. By Mardi Gras, the balloon rises to full view only to disappear the next morning. It succeeds because it's well-tethered, yet has the flexibility to shift with the wind."[1]

In his classic 1947 work, *Mardi Gras*, Robert Tallant, enthralled with the infectious Carnival spirit of New Orleans, expressed his wish that Mardi Gras be celebrated the world over:

Mardi Gras is very old, but it is also very young. It belongs to the past, yet also to the present and to the future. The face it wears now is not necessarily its last. It will exist in other forms, in other times, in other places. It would be wonderful if the clown in the grinning mask should appear on all the Main Streets of the world, if the blazing flambeaux and the rocking floats were everywhere, if everywhere there could be a season, or at least a day, devoted to laughter. And, besides all the other virtues of Mardi Gras, it also keeps a lot of men and women busy for a long time each year, preparing to play and for having fun, and thinking of these things, instead of devoting their time, their labor, and their thoughts towards ends more sinister.[2]

In the twenty-first century, Mardi Gras has yet to be celebrated on a worldwide stage as Tallant wished, but one thing is certain: scores of smaller cities, towns, and rural locales throughout the state of Louisiana observe the occasion, many on a large scale and with a long history, thereby offering the celebration to untold thousands of people who otherwise would not have enjoyed this unique American experience.

Though Carnival's oldest events are private balls staged in the aristocratic fashion of the nineteenth century, Carnival in Louisiana today is largely a production of, by, and for the common person. Parades are public events, open to viewing by all, and many organizers solicit participation. Balls and dances are available to the average citizen as well. As Louisianians of various walks of life participate in one or many expressions of Carnival, they collectively maintain the traditions and bring forth innovations that will continue to make Carnival and its climax of Mardi Gras among Louisiana's most appealing cultural gifts.

APPENDIX A
Sizing up the Crowds

Louisiana's cities and towns that stage Carnival parades take great pride in the large number of residents and visitors who attend each year's events. In some places, Carnival is the community's biggest activity of the year. Since the mid-twentieth century, the media, tourist bureaus, and law enforcement agencies have consistently ranked Louisiana's largest Fat Tuesday celebrations by attendance thus: first, Greater New Orleans; second, Lafayette; third, Houma and New Roads tied, with Thibodaux, Franklin, Morgan City, and Kaplan following. However, attendance at the Krewe of Krewes parade in Lake Charles has grown to allow that city to vie for second place statewide.

In any given year at any given parade, crowd estimates vary greatly from one opinion to another. Parade organizers tend to give high estimates while civic and law enforcement officials tend to give considerably lower figures. Published estimates of Fat Tuesday crowds have soared as high as 1.3 million for New Orleans' Uptown parade route; "1 million plus" for suburban Metairie; a staggering 800,000 for Lafayette (all in the *Baton Rouge Advocate*); 300,000 for Lake Charles (tourism calendar); 100,000 for New Roads (*Pointe Coupee Banner*) and Houma (*Advocate* and *Courier*); 50,000 for Franklin (*Acadiana Profile*), Thibodaux (*Daily Comet*), and Kaplan (*Advocate*); and 25,000 for Grand Marais (*Advocate*). More conservative and likely more accurate was the (Houma) *Bayou Catholic,* which in the mid-1990s estimated that "a million plus Mardi Gras goers" attend the parades each year throughout South Louisiana.[1]

Beginning in 1977, for several years James McLain, a University of New Orleans professor of economics, compiled a detailed summary of the financial impact of Carnival on Greater New Orleans. McLain's estimates of the Shrove Tuesday crowds in Orleans, Jefferson, and St. Bernard parishes combined rose from a "less than usual" 585,000 in 1997 to a record 943,000 in 2000. Within those few years, he determined the Shrove Tuesday crowds to be no longer the largest, but third in size for the Carnival season.

Even as estimates are usually on the liberal side—some downright fanciful—most observers agree that Carnival 2000 drew the largest crowds in history. This record remains through the first decade of the twenty-first century, as this celebration was succeeded by several years of inclement weather and the diaspora of city residents as well as fewer visitors coming in the wake of Hurricane Katrina.

An Estimation Formula

In the course of attending and studying the various Carnival events of my native Louisiana for more than forty years, I have become especially interested in estimating as accurately as possible the crowds that turn out each year for the parades. I have found that, in order to determine an approximate but fair count, one must physically survey the entire parade route during the parade's peak time. If that is not possible to do in person, film or photo imagery should be employed. My own surveys over more than twenty years have produced the following formula, based on length of parade route and average crowd depth:

1. Take the 5,280 feet in one mile, divide by two to allow a two-foot-wide standing room for each spectator, then multiply this figure by two to allow for spectators on both sides of the street.

2. Multiply the figure obtained above by the number of miles in the parade route.

3. Now for crowd depth, get the average number of rows of spectators along the entire route. For example, if the crowd is one row deep at its thinnest and five rows deep at its thickest, the average is three rows deep.

4. Multiply the figure in no. 2 above by the figure in no. 3; then round off to the nearest 5,000, and you have a simple, unbiased crowd count that may be applied to any Carnival parade.

Application of this formula to events with record crowds in or just prior to 2016, which was marked by fine weather, yields the following results.

In New Orleans, on the Saturday before Mardi Gras, where maximum attendance along the six-mile, Uptown-Downtown parade route ranges from six to twenty rows deep, a calculation based on the above formula yields a total of 410,000 spectators. The number of Carnival-goers in the city increases when taking into consideration the French

Thousands of visitors from near and far line the streets of New Orleans and other Louisiana cities and towns each Carnival season.
(Courtesy Louisiana Office of Tourism)

Quarter revelers not attending the parades, a calculation not easily arrived at owing to the fluidity of the French Quarter crowd, but certainly in the tens of thousands.

In Lafayette, on Mardi Gras, where peak attendance along the four-mile parade route varies from one to twelve rows deep, the above formula yields a total of 140,000 spectators.

In Lake Charles, on Mardi Gras, where maximum attendance along the four-and-a-quarter-mile route ranges from one to twelve rows deep, the formula yields nearly 155,000 spectators, thereby surpassing Lafayette's traditional claim of second place.

In Houma, on Mardi Gras, where the heaviest attendance along the four-and-a-half-mile route ranges from one to six rows deep, the result is 85,000 parade-goers.

In New Roads, on Mardi Gras, where maximum attendance along the three-mile route varies from one to nine rows deep, the formula yields a total of 80,000 spectators.

And in Thibodaux, on the Sunday before Mardi Gras, where peak attendance along the three-and-a-half-mile route ranges from one to three rows deep, the formula yields a total of 35,000 onlookers.

Crowds are smaller and the calculations thereby lower, of course, during celebrations marked by unfavorable weather conditions.

Noted New Orleans chronicler Arthur Hardy has long shared my doubts about crowd estimates for Carnival parades and, even more so, for the New Orleans Saints Super Bowl victory parade in 2010, billed as the largest ever in the city center, with 800,000 in attendance, forty rows deep in some areas.

Regardless, the sheer number of individuals who turn out for Louisiana's various Carnival parades, many defying inclement weather to do so, season after season, is undeniable evidence of the festive season's popularity and its rank as one of the largest annual events in the nation, if not the world.

APPENDIX B
Additional Resources

Information about Louisiana's many Carnival festivities is available in abundance from various sources, including print, Internet, tourist bureaus, and museums.

Published Information

One of the best-known and most extensive previews of each year's Carnival parades and related events in Greater New Orleans is *Arthur Hardy's Mardi Gras Guide,* an annual publication by Arthur Hardy Enterprises since 1977. This resource, likewise rich in historical feature articles and imagery, may be purchased in bookstores and other retail outlets, as well as online.

Listings of each year's parades in the cities and towns outside of New Orleans may be found in the Louisiana Office of Tourism's complimentary annual "Calendar of Events" brochure or on its web site, as well as in the newspapers and other periodicals of the individual communities.

The potential parade-goer is advised to search online for the name of a particular krewe, community, parish, or tourism agency to find sites replete with information concerning parades and related events, no-alcohol zones, access for the physically challenged, family-friendly options, and so forth.

In addition to the sources cited in the bibliography, the following printed works offer pertinent information on the history of Carnival in Louisiana.

Costello, Brian J. *Chronicles of Carnival: A History of the New Roads Mardi Gras.* New Roads, La.: Pointe Coupee, 1999.

———. *Rolling for Charity: A History of the New Roads Lions Carnival.* New Roads, La.: New Roads Lions Club, 2004.

Gill, James. *Lords of Misrule: Mardi Gras and the Politics of Race in New Orleans.* Jackson: University Press of Mississippi, 1997.

Laborde, Errol. *Krewe: The Early New Orleans Mardi Gras, Comus to Zulu.* New Orleans: Carnival Press, 2007 and subsequent editions.

———. *Marched the Day God: A History of the Rex Organization.* New Orleans: School of Design, 1999.

———. *Mardi Gras: Chronicles of the New Orleans Carnival.* New Orleans: Pelican, 2013.

Mitchell, Reid. *All on a Mardi Gras Day: Episodes in the History of New Orleans Carnival.* Cambridge, Mass.: Harvard University Press, 1999.

The Mardi Gras Museum in Lake Charles has breathtaking exhibits of costumes and regalia, offering visitors a year-round view of Carnival splendor.
(Courtesy Louisiana Office of Tourism)

O'Neill, Rosary. *New Orleans Carnival Krewes: The History, Spirit and Secrets of Mardi Gras.* Charleston, S.C.: History Press, 2014.

Schindler, Henri. *Mardi Gras Treasures: Costume Designs of the Golden Age.* Gretna, La.: Pelican, 2002 and subsequent editions.

———. *Mardi Gras Treasures: Float Designs of the Golden Age.* Gretna, La.: Pelican, 2001.

———. *Mardi Gras Treasures: Invitations of the Golden Age.* Gretna, La.: Pelican, 2000.

———. *Mardi Gras Treasures: Jewelry of the Golden Age.* Gretna, La.: Pelican, 2006 and subsequent editions.

Smith, Michael. *Mardi Gras Indians.* Gretna, La.: Pelican, 1994.

Vaz, Kim Marie. *The "Baby Dolls": Breaking the Race and Gender Barriers of the New Orleans Mardi Gras Tradition.* Baton Rouge: Louisiana State University Press, 2013.

Mardi Gras Exhibits

Carnival devotees need not wait for each year's season to view the glamour and diversity of the annual celebration, past or present. From robes and regalia that have lost little of their luster since old-line nineteenth-century balls, to floats and costumes currently under construction, museums and other venues in Louisiana have Carnival on display year-round.

The Louisiana State Museum features a fine interactive exhibit in New Orleans' historic Presbytère on Jackson Square, where the glory of Carnival past is related through the theme "Mardi Gras: It's Carnival Time in Louisiana."

The Backstreet Cultural Museum at 1116 St. Claude Avenue in New Orleans' Faubourg Tremé houses the largest display of Mardi Gras Indian costumes and photos, in addition to exhibits devoted to music and jazz funerals.

Blaine Kern's Mardi Gras World at 1380 Port of New Orleans Place, in the Uptown section of the city, is the world's largest float-construction facility. Visitors are guided through the huge premises on a historical tour of the annual celebration and float building, with king cake and coffee offered as complimentary dessert.

The House of Dance and Feathers cultural center at 1317 Tupelo Street in the Ninth Ward of New Orleans features memorabilia related to the Mardi Gras Indians, Baby Dolls, and other African American contributions to Carnival history and diversity.

New Orleans' oldest restaurant, Antoine's, at 713 St. Louis Street in the French Quarter, has been the scene of many of Carnival's most elaborate krewe functions. Rooms are named for individual krewes and showcase their respective regalia, ball invitations and favors, photographs, and other priceless items from the late nineteenth through the twentieth century. These luxurious chambers are named the Rex, Proteus, and Twelfth Night Revelers dining rooms and the Hermes Bar; they are open to public viewing when not engaged by private parties.

Famed Arnaud's Restaurant at 813 Bienville Street, also in the French Quarter, houses one of the city's best-known displays of Carnival costumes and regalia, much of which was designed for and worn by late restaurant owner Germaine Cazenave Wells and her family. Mrs. Wells, daughter of restaurant founder Arnaud "Count" Cazenave, was queen of more than twenty-two New Orleans Carnival balls from 1937 to 1968, and her father was king at least four times.

On the Northshore of Lake Pontchartrain, the Slidell Mardi Gras Museum is one of the newest facilities to highlight Carnival year-round. Located at 2020 First Street, to the rear of the city's old jail, the facility houses hundreds of costumes, scepters, goblets, and scrapbooks of hundreds of photographs from past parades compiled by director Arriollia "Bonnie" Vanney.

In downtown Baton Rouge, the state's Capitol Park Museum at 660 North Fourth Street features displays and interactive videos devoted to Carnival, with emphasis on the capital city and Acadiana.

The Mardi Gras Museum of Imperial Calcasieu, located in the Central School Arts & Humanities Center at 809 Kirby Street in Lake

Charles, houses the reputedly largest collection of Mardi Gras costumes in the American South.

In Morgan City, the Mardi Gras Museum & Cypress Manor, housed in a lovely 1906 residence at 715 Second Street, includes Carnival artifacts and memorabilia in its display of local history.

The Pointe Coupee Parish Library at 201 Claiborne Street in New Roads houses one of the most complete sets of Carnival regalia, that of 1906 New Orleans Queen of Carnival and library founder, Adrienne Lawrence, as well as her collection of period ball favors and invitations. Items from former New Roads Lions Carnival royalty are also featured in the exhibit, and the library's Historic Materials Collection contains vintage films and hundreds of images of New Roads' parading tradition.

In keeping with the spread and growth of Carnival in North Louisiana, the Mardi Gras Museum at 2101 East Texas Street in Bossier City pays homage to the perennial celebration with a local emphasis.

NOTES

Introduction

1. Arthur Burton LaCour, *New Orleans Masquerade: Chronicles of Carnival* (New Orleans: Pelican, 1952), 11–12.
2. Ibid., 12.
3. Arthur Hardy, *Mardi Gras in New Orleans: An Illustrated History* (Mandeville, La.: Arthur Hardy Enterprises, 2009), 6.
4. T. C. De Leon, *Our Creole Carnivals: Their Origin, History, Progress and Results 1830–1890* (Mobile, Ala.: Gossip Printing Co., 1890), 14.
5. New Orleans *Daily Picayune,* February 25, 1914.

1. The Old-Line Four: Comus, Rex, Momus, and Proteus

1. *Daily Picayune,* February 24, 1909.

2. The Zulu Social Aid and Pleasure Club

1. Robert Tallant, *Mardi Gras* (Garden City, N.Y.: Doubleday & Co., 1948), 249.
2. "History of the Zulu Social Aid & Pleasure Club," www.zulu.com/history (accessed September 9, 2015).

6. Walking Clubs and Other Street Traditions

1. Barbra Barnett, "'Hey You! Anti-Semite!' A Jewish Krewe Does Mardi Gras," *Religion Dispatches,* USC Annenberg, religiondispatches.org/hey-you-anti-semite-a-jewish-krewe-does-mardi-gras (accessed May 1, 2016).

9. Courir de Mardi Gras

1. Harnett T. Kane, *The Bayous of Louisiana* (New York: William Morrow & Co., 1941), 305.

11. Terrebonne and Lafourche Parishes

1. "Mardi Gras Guide," www.houmatimes.com/gumbo/eedition (accessed Jan. 30, 2016). Emphasis added.

13. New Roads

1. DeBretton Cohn, "A Bow to the Town of New Roads," *The Register* (Baton Rouge), February 18, 1956.

14. Baton Rouge

1. Pam Bordelon, "What Is a Krewe?" *Baton Rouge Advocate,* January 17, 2010, 1D.
2. "History," Mystick Krewe of Louisianians, Washington Mardi Gras Ball, mkofl.com/heritage (accessed February 29, 2016).

Epilogue

1. "Krewes News," *New Orleans Magazine,* www.myneworleans.com (accessed February 4, 2016).
2. Tallant, *Mardi Gras,* xi.

Appendix A: Sizing up the Crowds

1. *Houma Bayou Catholic,* February 1997.

BIBLIOGRAPHY

Louisiana Newspapers and Guides

Acadiana Profile (Lafayette).

The Advertiser (Lafayette).

The Advocate (Baton Rouge).

American Press (Lake Charles).

Arthur Hardy's Mardi Gras Guide (New Orleans).

Avoyelles Journal (Marksville).

Banner-Tribune (Franklin).

Daily Comet (Thibodaux).

Daily Iberian (New Iberia).

Daily Picayune (New Orleans).

Daily Town Talk (Alexandria).

Daily World (Opelousas).

The Derrick (Oil City).

Gumbo Guide (Houma).

Houma Bayou Catholic.

Houma Courier.

The Item (New Orleans).

Louisiana Traveler.

Louisiana Weekly (New Orleans).

Morning Advocate (Baton Rouge).

Natchitoches Times.

News-Star (Monroe).

Pointe Coupee Banner (New Roads).

St. Mary Banner (Franklin).

St. Mary–Franklin Banner Tribune (Franklin).

Shreveport Times.

State-Times (Baton Rouge).

Teche News (St. Martinville).
Times-Picayune (New Orleans).
Weekly Iberian (New Iberia).
Weekly Messenger (St. Martinville).
Winn Parish Enterprise (Winnfield).

Books

Blackburn, Florence, and Fay G. Brown, eds. *Franklin Through the Years.* Franklin, La., 1972.

Caillot, Marc-Antoine. *A Company Man: The Remarkable French-Atlantic Voyage of a Clerk for the Company of the Indies.* Ed. Erin M. Greenwald. New Orleans: Historic New Orleans Collection, 2013.

De Leon, T. C. *Our Creole Carnivals: Their Origin, History, Progress and Results, 1830–1890.* Mobile, Ala.: Gossip Printing Co., 1890.

Dufour, Charles L., and Leonard V. Huber. *If Ever I Cease to Love: One Hundred Years of Rex, 1872–1971.* New Orleans: School of Design, 1970.

Hardy, Arthur. *Mardi Gras in New Orleans: An Illustrated History.* Mandeville, La.: Arthur Hardy Enterprises, Inc., 2009.

Kane, Harnett T. *The Bayous of Louisiana.* New York: William Morrow & Co., 1941.

LaCour, Arthur Burton. *New Orleans Masquerade: Chronicles of Carnival.* New Orleans: Pelican Publishing Co., 1952.

Lindhal, Carl, and Carolyn Ware. *Cajun Mardi Gras Masks.* Jackson: University Press of Mississippi, 1997.

Love, Frances, and John Love. *Allons à L'Acadie.* Lafayette, La.: Tribune Printing Plant, 1957.

Ross, Nora Mae Wittler. *Mardi Gras in Calcasieu Parish: A Pictorial History.* Sulphur, La.: Wise Printing Co., 1991.

Tallant, Robert. *Mardi Gras.* Garden City, N.Y.: Doubleday & Co., 1948.

Young, Perry. *The Mystick Krewe: Chronicles of Comus and His Kin.* New Orleans: Carnival Press, 1931.

Articles

Barnett, Barbra. "'Hey You! Anti-Semite!' A Jewish Krewe Does Mardi Gras. *Religion Dispatches,* USC Annenberg, religiondispatches.org/hey-you-anti -semite-a-jewish-krewe-does-mardi-gras/.

BIBLIOGRAPHY

Bordelon, Pam. "What Is a Krewe?" *Baton Rouge Advocate,* January 17, 2010, 1D.

Cohn, DeBretton. "A Bow to the Town of New Roads," *The Register* (Baton Rouge), February 18, 1956.

Oster, Harry, and Reven Reed. "Country Mardi Gras in Louisiana," *Louisiana Folklore Miscellany,* January 1960.

Web Sites

alexmardigras.com

joanofarcparade.org

kingcakefestival.org

livinglifecajunstyle.com/mardi-gras-2014-in-gueydan-la

louisiana.kitchenandculture.com/louisiana-mardi-gras-parade-schedule

visitlakecharles.org/events-festivals/mardigras

www.gomardigras.com

www.louisianatravel.com/articles/mardi-gras-shreveport-bossier-city

www.mardigras.com

www.monroe-westmonroe.org

www.myneworleans-com/Louisiana-Life

www.mystic-krewe-de-saint-denis.com

www.pineville.net

www.zulu.com